AP
Sociology

AF529314

THE CHANGING FACE OF RURAL INDIA

S. Asaithambi
A. Mohamed Abdullah
N. Kannan

ABHIJEET PUBLICATIONS
DELHI 110094

ABHIJEET PUBLICATIONS
2/46 Tukhmeerpur Extension
Delhi-110 094
Phone: 011-22960492, 65698474
E-mail: abhijeetpublication@gmail.com

THE CHANGING FACE OF RURAL INDIA

First Published 2008

© Authors

ISBN 978-81-89886-56-1

[All rights reserved. No part of this publication may be reproduced, copied, stored in a retrieval system, transmitted or used in any form or by any means, whether electronic, mechanical, photocopying, recording or otherwise, without the prior permission from the author or publishers, except for a brief quotations in critical articles or reviews.]

PRINTED IN INDIA

Published by J.K. Singh for Abhijeet Publications, Delhi-110 094, Lasertypeset by Gaurav Graphics, New Delhi and Printed at Himanshu Printers, Delhi.

Dedicated to
Our Beloved Parents

Preface

Mahatma Gandhi observed that India lives in Rural Areas. If you want to improve the whole part of India your attention must simply goes to Rural oriented plans. This book made an attempt to analyse the real position of rural India in nowadays and also through lights the detailed structure of the rural society and hence also focuses the rural-urban divide, various policies and programmes of rural development like health care, programmes, self-employment programmes, practices and methods of rural marketing and rural energy and other related rural energy issue and so on.

Of late India has witnessed rapid changes in the countryside and rural areas. With the onset of IT revolution, the mobile penetration, cable TV penetration etc. has helped to bring greater changes in hitherto idyllic unspoilt countryside. Forces of marketing and consumerism are also operating and one can find all kinds of goods and services available in small mofussil towns as well. This book explores the changing face of rural India. It is hoped that this book will fulfill a lacunae in the field of rural studies and will help students, researchers, academicians, NGOs and policy makers as well.

AUTHORS

Contents

1

The Changing Face of Rural India

Introduction

Spread across 500,000 village, with an average population of 1,100, rural villages were long imagined by city dwellers as primitive, impoverished and irrelevant, something to drive past on the way to something else.

That is no longer the case. A new prosperity is sprouting in rural India, with tens of millions entering the pressure-cooker-and-television-owning class and tens of thousands becoming sippers of Scotch, owners of premium tractors and drivers of multiple sedans.

The opening of this new frontier of consumer demand from 700 million people could tip India's role in the global economy from seller to buyer, from a vendor of outsourced skills to a source of consumers for the world's wares. Multinational corporations, from Coca-Cola to Nokia, appear increasingly keep to understand Indian villagers.

At the extreme of the trend are the "crorepatis," Hindi for those making the equivalent of $220,000 or more a year. Here in the northern state of Haryana, rural dwellers are now nearly twice as likely to be crorepatis as city dwellers in Bangalore, the high-technology hub, according to the National Council for Applied Economic Research, the leading collector of data on rural India.

It may be a trickle, but India's urban prosperity is flowing to the countryside. And well-to-do village like Hasangarh are early testing grounds of whether the benefits of India's economic makeover and opening to the world will flow to its villages, many of them living in its very poorest rural nooks.

The transformation of such villages will also add fuel to the debate over democracy's influence on economic development. India has been faulted for growing more lethargically than China, in part because of its democracy.

But the new rural prosperity suggests that the high cost of democracy also has a hidden benefits. By compelling each politician to deliver results to his own narrow constituency, democracy spreads economic change more thinly. But that in turn broadens the consensus in favour of change, perhaps making liberalization more sustainable in India than in China, said Yasheng Huang, a Chinese-born scholar at the Massachusetts Institute of Technology and an expert on the two countries.

"In China in the 1990s, you have a combination of a leadership who had an urban bias and of an authoritarian system that suppressed the voices of the poor, and the end result was the suppressed the voices of the poor, and the end result was the rising rural–urban disparity and the high level of social tensions," Huang said in an e-mail interview.

"If you have an urban bias, then it is better to have a democracy because then the voters can rise up to correct that bias, especially, as in India, where poor people actively vote".

In China, a widening income gap between town and country is worrying officials. But in India, the gap is narrowing. In 1990, for every $100 earned by an Indian villager, an urbanite made $82 more. Today, the difference has dropped to $56.

Yet the new rural riches are far from ending poverty. In India, 390 million peoples still live on $1 a day or less.

What is changing is the nature of the rich-poor divide. That divide was once synonymous with the urban-rural split. The only way to get rich was to live in town, and to reside in the country was to be bound to interminable poverty.

But increasingly, the rural economy is a microcosm of the national economy with its own rich and poor. The rural rich are 1,000 times as likely as the rural poor to won a motorcycle, 100 times as likely to own a colour television and 25 times as likely to own a pressure cooker, according to a survey of 96,000 rural households by the research council.

That distribution of wealth may or may not be equitable. But in creating the possibility of making it in rural India itself, the new rural prosperity is transforming rural India's image from economic nonentity to emerging market within the emerging market.

India's 700 million villagers now account for the majority of consumer spending in the country, more than $100 billion a year. Millions step into consumerism each year, graduating from the economics of necessity to the economics of gratification, buying themselves motorcycles, televisions, transistor radios and pressure cookers.

Diverse forces are fuelling the trend. The government has invested billions of dollars in development, including road building and rural electrification, and has forced banks to lend to farmers. Hearty monsoons have fattened farmers' profits. Widening educational access has helped farmers' children to get city jobs and send money home.

With the private sector booming, industry and services have overtaken farming to account for 54 per cent of rural income.

"Basically, what we are observing is the impact of liberalization, which started in 1992" said an economist and senior fellow. "The impact on the smaller towns and rural areas is happening now".

Hasangarh belongs to a new India: neither rural nor urban but something in between. The village, two-hour drive from New Delhi, is one such island in a rural sea, surrounded on all sides by swaying grass, wooden buffalo carts and scrawny farmers.

But upon arriving, there is a feeling of being in a village without villagers. The roads are made of mud, and the residents still sit on their doorsteps, biding their time. But here is a village where $20,000 dowries are paid not in cattle but in televisions and sedans. Here is a village where residents one generation removed from illiteracy now belong to that worldwide class of people who watch global news events as they unfold.

Here, too, is a village where the rural riches are creating winners and losers.

Many here have been hurt by the privatization of bloated state-owned enterprises and the opening of the agricultural industry to global competition. Part-time and freelance work is ever more common, replacing respectable salaried jobs. Here, and across India, most of the workers are farmers or landless labourers. For India's rivers to extend to them, economists say, will require a revolution in farm productivity; drastic improvements in infrastructure like roads, irrigation and electricity; and the proliferation of labour-intensive factories to absorb surplus labour from the farms. None seems an immediate likelihood.

But also in this village, as is increasingly true nationwide, being rural is no longer a life sentence of poverty. For rich and middling farmers alike, education is within closer reach.

Ten years ago, the area had three schools; it now has five. And ever more students travel to small towns or even Delhi to pursue higher education after high school.

That widening access to education assists what is perhaps the pivotal shift in the economics of rural households: diversification.

Farmers verging on retirement, sensing the decline of their own profession, are treating their children like stocks in a portfolio, sending them out into different vocations so as to minimize the risk of any one collapsing.

Across India, the shift is palpable. Around one-fifth of village households, now generate their primary income from a salaried job or a small business like a village store, not from farming. And it is these new jobs that are driving rural demand, with that one-fifth segment accounting for 60 percent of rural purchases of refrigerators, for example.

Some analysts, however, while welcoming the growing rural prosperity, say that the government still needs to do more to address the disparity between town and country.

But much of the new rural wealth was the result of a trickle-down effect from the cities, rather than a bottom-up agricultural revolution, which was the only sustainable way to put most Indians to productive work.

Seventy-five per cent of your population in rural India has not been addressed. Unless you do that, the huge tail will be left behind. The government has to create a continuum between urban and rural.

Some Questions and their Answers

How Much Has Rural India Changed in its Aspirations, Attitude and Consumption?

Rural India has changed tremendously. The data published by the National Council of Applied Economic Research shows that in the last ten years, the income of rural India has grown several-fold. There is a definite shift from middle to upper middle class and from lower to middle class segments.

Is the Shift Due to the Growth in Indian Agriculture?

For the last 10 consecutive years, we have had good monsoons. So, agriculture is prospering. Of course, the last couple of years have gone bad.

Another interesting aspect is, today rural India is no 100 per cent dependent on a agrarian economy. Unlike in the past where the ratio between those who involved in agriculture and in other business was 75-25, today the estimated ratio is 50:50, if not 60:40.

So today, 50-60 per cent of the rural population is involved in other businesses. A lot of people belonging to the second generation are getting white-collar jobs in nearby towns. So, there is a growing middle class with a monthly income in rural India and it is a drastic change from the past where their income was totally dependent on the monsoon, cropping season, etc.

This has resulted in a definite growth in the prosperity level in rural India. Of course, there are still a lot of poor people, especially the agricultural labourers. But there is a growing middle class with regular income and the rural rich are becoming richer.

Is the Urban-Rural Divide in India Thinning Now?

The urban-rural divide is still there, but the divide between urban and rural India is thinning among the top segment of rural India. The rural rich are almost like urban India.

Rural India is like a pyramid. The top of the pyramid is occupied by the rich farmers and businessmen. They may constitute around 5 per cent of the population. The next level belongs to those with a regular income and the base of the pyramid is occupied by the vast majority of the people who are daily wage labourers.

So we cannot say that the urban-rural divide has melted. It is still there. But there is hope with the growing emphasis on education.

How Would One Categories Different Parts of Rural India?

In India, we have the developed rural India and undeveloped rural India. Punjab, Haryana, Tamil Nadu, Andhra Pradesh, Kerala and parts of Maharashtra come under the developed rural India but the rest of the states are undeveloped where power, infrastructure, etc. are big problems.

The prosperity of Kerala has come from the NRI income and not from agriculture. Today, there is hardly any village in Kerala.

Tamil Nadu is prosperous as power and good roads are available. All the villages with proper infrastructure have developed. In such villages, people also have better access to towns and cities.

What are the Major Reasons for the Change in the Lifestyle of the Developed Rural India?

Televisions has done wonders to rural India. Today, especially in the south, the penetration of satellite television is very high, which is around 50 per cent unlike 25-30 per cent in the rest of the country.

These people may not be literate in the true sense but they know what is happening around the world because of television. They know how the rest of the country live.

Is Television Driving the Aspirations or Rural India?

Definitely, the rural youth today is an important trigger in changing the profile of rural India. About 40 per cent of the graduates coming out of Indian universities today are doing very well.

Their aspirations are similar to the urban youth, and it gets reflected in their eagerness to earn more and live better. So, if there is a problem in agriculture, they do something else. They ensure that they have steady flow of income.

It has been reported that by 2009-10, the number of urban households is projected to grow by 4 per cent, while rural households are expected to grow by 11 per cent.

Are Developmental Initiatives Reaching Rural India?

The total expenditure of urban India is almost equal to what has been spent by rural India. But what is being spent by urban India. But what is being spent by urban India is being done by only a small percentage of the population.

About 25 per cent of the urban India is spending as much as 75 per cent of what rural India is spending. This shows that potential exists in rural India. There is a huge market waiting to be tapped in rural India.

So the Corporate World and MNCs Cannot Ignore Rural India

Yes, they cannot afford to ignore rural India. Unfortunately, they are only talking about it, they are not investing enough to get the maximum mileage out of it.

For them, rural India is an unknown entity even today, and it calls for a lot of investment. Initially, the ratio between investment and returns will not be the same as you see in urban India. For urban India, one television spot is enough but it's not so in rural India. You have to slog it out there.

But eventually, you will get the returns. In today's corporate world, all the managers, especially those working in the MNCs depend on their quarterly results. They only look at what give them immediate success. Freebies have no meaning in rural India. You have to given value for money for the brand you are selling.

How Long Can the Corporate World Ignore Rural India?

You will not be able to survive without rural India in future. One company that conquered the rural market 50 years ago and has consistently penetrating rural areas is Hindustan Lever.

About 50-55 per cent of their sales come from the rural market. Even today, they are constantly innovating and improvising. And Hindustan Lever is marketing directly in the rural markets.

The success of Cavin Kare has become very notable case study. It is a company that began in a small way. It started the Chic shampoo sachet for 50 paise when shampoo was available at Rs. 1, and it revolutionized the market.

The sachet pack itself was a novel way of attracting the rural market. Now, it has conquered the rural market all over India. They are giving a run for Hindustan Lever's investments, as they have understood the local market very well and communicate in their language. Now, Maruti is also seriously looking at rural India.

According to a report, between June 2002 and December 2003, rural per capita consumption expenditure grew by 11.5 per cent while the urban expenditure grew by 9.6 per cent.

Yes, there is a tremendous potential for consumer durables like television sets, refrigerators, air-conditioners and household appliances in rural India.

After the basic needs of food, cloth and shelter, they are looking at how to live better.

Television is the most sought after consumer item in rural India followed by two wheelers. Gradually, they are moving to small cars like Maruti and that's what Maruti is trying to exploit.

Village Culture and Tourism

Indian city dwellers often refer nostalgically to "simple village life". City artists portray colourfully garbed village women gracefully carrying water pots on their heads, and writers describe isolated rural settlements unsullied by the complexities of modern urban civilization. Social scientists of the past wrote of Indian villages as virtually self-sufficient communities with few ties to the outside world.

Rajasthani Village Tourism

Far from the royal cities of the state, the village of Rajasthan hold their own distinct charm. Though they usually lack any attraction in form of forts, palaces, gardens and wild life sanctuaries, yet they are worth visiting for the simple reason that they present the life of Rajasthan at its most basic. The rural life of Rajasthan reflects the determination of the people to survive in even most difficult of circumstances. For a tourist visiting Rajasthan for the first time, it is actually difficult to find a village in the vast stretches of barren land. It is only when a herd of cattle is seen around that the tourist gets an inkling of a village in closeby area. Many a times, interestingly, even these signs are not seen and the tourists acknowledge the existence of a village only upon entering it.

Once in the village, tourists realize that they have reached a place that is most simple and has perhaps remained static over last many years. A simple village has a group of people living in circular thatched roof huts with walls made up of plaster of clay, cow dung, ad hay. The houses are branches of a nettle-like shrub. The sharp thorns of boundaries ensures that the cattle do not leave the premises on their own. Bigger houses can be found in larger villages only and they mostly belong to affluent Zamindar families. The only decoration that can be seen in the simplest of houses are in form of a texture in the plaster in the façade or designer patterns at the entrance and outside the kitchen.

The people of these villages belong to different communities and are segregated according to the nature of their profession. These people have deep religious faith that help them survive in this immensely difficult landscape. Each house has a separate corner reserved specially for worship. Every morning, the villagers pray before a calendar image of the god to bless them as always and protect them from all sinister eyes. Quite often the people in the villages are lead by a Rajput.

The major meal of the family is at the time of dinner when freshly baked bread and porridge along with yogurt curry called karhi and vegetables like dried beans are taken. Breakfast and lunch are very frugal. The meals are generally vegetarian. Non-vegetarian dishes are restricted to only special occasions and festivals.

For a tourist, the ideal way to visit a village is quiet obviously on the back of a camel. The most interesting sights that grabs the attention of tourists are the women around the community well. Dressed in colourful attires, these women present a more lively attitude of the Rajasthanis. Close by is a group of people discussing important issues relating to their village or general topics like politics. Lastly, there are children either studying in an open air school or running around with complete freedom. Theses sights do not sound as attractive, however, they have a genuine innocence hidden beneath that is heartening. And, the gesture of the villagers towards their guests is extremely hospitable. Tourists can get a better insight into the life of rural Rajasthan by interacting with these people.

Himachal Pradesh Village Tourism

Kinnaur Village

Located in the dizzying heights of the Himalayas, with passes that remain closed for six months linking them with the rest of the world, Kinnaur, Spiti & Lahaul were till now a forbidden land. Only a chosen few were granted permission to visit this secret world, officials, Moravian missionaries who settled here in 1853 and a few mountaineers.

. Now this area has been opened for the daring and adventurous to discover what had been hidden from the world for centuries.

From the riotous green of the Sangla Valley files with orchards of apricots, peaches, chilgozas and apples to the magnificent desolation of the Hangrang Valley, Mother Nature's portrait is an ever changing one in Kinnaur. This land lying on the ancient trade route between India and Tibet, ringed by the majestic mountain of the Himalayan and Dhauladhar rang is the land of plenty.

The gushing rivers of Kinnaur abound in Trout—the angler's prize catch, their waters have over the centuries chiselled beautiful gorges across this picturesque land and nurtured one of the most unique societies on there banks in the lush land live the descendants of the Kinners—the demi gods of the Hindu pantheon, whose deeds have been immortalized in epics and the poems of ancient Sanskrit poets.

Village Tourism in Kerala

As you travel forward in your comfortable car, travel backwards in time to places where the way of life has not changed and where everything is still built by hand, made by hand and created by hand. Visit people untouched by western ideals, computers or modern "necessities".

In the villages of Kerala you can enjoy true Indian hospitality, where the guest is god. The colours of the turbans and the saris of the women are in stark contrast to the often parched backdrop of the landscape. You will be amazed by the elegant way these village women carry a myriad of pots on their heads and their incredible dresses.

The women cover the outside of their houses with mud and then paint them with intricate designs, using only their hands and a past made of lime. Accommodation is even so, comfortable for the traveller. Many houses previously owned by the local gentry, are now being run as small hotels. Even though modern amenities are provided, they have lost nothing of their originality and charm. This area is dotted with villages, filled with beautifully painted huts, all easily visited within a day or two.

Your hosts will be proud to show you around the village, where you can see many artisans at work. Stone cutting, carpentry, inlay work, textile block printing, potters at their wheels; so many crafts which have long been lost in western society. Some of Kerala's most interesting features can be seen during these tours. These tours can be combined with visits to Tribal villages and also with tours to major places of interest. For those having visited India already, a village tour will show you yet again, a different face of this fascinating country.

2

Rural Indian Problems and Government Schemes

Anti Poverty Schemes

The government has initiated, sustained, and refined many programmes since independence to help the poor attain self sufficiency in food production. Probably the most important initiative has been the supply of basic commodities, particularly food at controlled prices, available throughout the country. The poor spend about 80 percent of their income on food while the rest of the population spends more than 60 per cent. The price of food is a major determinant of wage scales. Often when food prices rise sharply, rioting and looking follow. Until the late 1970s, the government frequently had difficulty obtaining adequate grain supplies in years of poor harvests. During those times, states with surpluses of grain were cordoned off to force partial sales to public agencies and to keep private traders from shipping grain to deficit areas to secure very high prices; state government in surplus-grain areas were often less than cooperative. After the late 1970s, the central government, by holding reserve stocks and importing grain adequately and early, maintained sufficient supplies to meet the increased demand during drought years. It also provided more remunerative prices to farmers.

In rural Indian areas, the government has undertaken programmes to mitigate the worst effects of adverse monsoon rainfall, which affects not only farmers but village artisans and traders when the price of grain rises. The government has supplied water by financing well digging and, since the early 1980s, by power-assisted well drilling; rescinded land taxes from drought areas; tried to maintain stable food prices; and provided food through a food-for-work programmes is often a secondary consideration, but useful projects sometimes result. Employment is offered at a low daily wage, usually paid in grain, the rationale being that only the truly needy will take jobs at such low pay.

In the 1980s and early 1990s, Indian government programmes attempted to provide basic needs at stable, low prices; to increase income through pricing and regulations, such as supplying water from irrigation works, fertilizer, and other inputs; to foster location of industry in backward areas; to increase access to basic social services, such as education, health, and potable water supply; and to help needy groups and deprived areas. The total money spent on such programmes for the poor was not discernible from the budget data, but probably exceeded 10 percent of planned budget outlays.

India has had a number of anti-poverty programmes since the early 1960s. These include, among others, the National Rural Employment Programme and the Rural Landless Employment Guarantee Programme. The National Rural Employment Programme evolved in FY 1983 to address the plight of the hard-core rural poor by expanding employment opportunities and building the rural infrastructure as a means of encouraging rapid economic growth. There were many problems with the implementation of these and other schemes, but observers credit them with helping reduce poverty. To improve the effectiveness of the National Rural Employment Programme, in 1989 it was combined with the Rural Landless Employment Guarantee Programme and renamed Jawahar Rozgar Yojana, or Jawahar Employment Plan.

State government are important participants in anti-poverty programmes. The constitution assigns responsibility to the states in a number of matters, including ownership, redistribution, improvement, and taxation of land. State governments implement most central government programmes concerned with land reform and the situation of small landless farmers. The central government tries to establish programmes and norms among the states and union territories, but implementation has often remained at the lower bureaucratic levels. In some matters concerning subsoil rights and irrigation projects, the central government exerts political and financial leverage to obtain its objectives, but the states sometimes modify or retard the impact of central government policies and programmes.

Development Planning

Planning in India dates back to the 1930s. Even before independence, the colonial government had established a planning board that lasted fro 1944 to 1946. Private industrialists and economists published three development plans in 1944. India's leaders adopted the principle of formal economic planning soon after independence as an effective way to intervene in the economy to foster growth and social justice.

The Planning Commission was established in 1950. Responsible only to the prime minister, the commission is independent of the cabinet. The prime minister is chairperson of the commission, and the minister of state with independent charge for planning and programme implementation serves as deputy chairperson. A staff drafts national plans under the guidance of the commission; draft plans are presented fro approval to the National Development Council, which consists of the Planning

Commission and the chief ministers of the states. The council can make changes in the draft plan. After council approval, the draft is presented to the cabinet ad subsequently to Parliament, whose approval makes the plan an operating document for central and state government.

The First Five Year Plan (FY 1951-55) attempted to stimulate balanced economic development while correcting imbalances caused by World War II and partition. Agriculture, including projects that combined irrigation and power generation, received priority. By contrast, the Second Five-Year basic, heavy industries in the public sector, and improvement of the economic infrastructure. The plan also stressed social goals, such as more equal distribution of income and extension of the benefits of economic development to the large number of disadvantaged people. The Third Five-Year Plan (FY 1961-65) aimed at a substantial rise in national ad per capita income while expanding the industrial base and rectifying the neglect of agriculture in the previous plan. The third plan called for national income to grow at a rate of more than 5 percent a year; self-sufficiency in food grains was anticipated in the mid-1960s.

Economic difficulties disrupted the planning process in the mid-1960s. In 1962, when a brief war was fought with China on the Himalayan frontier, agricultural output was stagnating, industrial production was considerably below expectation, and the economy was growing at about half of the planned rate. Defence expenditures increased sharply, and the increased foreign aid needed to maintain development expenditures eventually provided 28 percent of public development spending. Midway through the third plan, it was clear that its goals could not be achieved. Food prices rose in 1963, causing rioting and looting of grain warehouses in 1964.

War with Pakistan in 1965 sharply reduced the foreign aid available. Successive severe droughts in 1965 and 1966 further disrupted the economy and planning. Three annual plans guided development between FY 1966 and FY 1968 while plan policies and strategies were reevaluated. Immediate attention centred on increasing agricultural growth, stimulating exports, and searching for efficient uses of industrial assets. Agriculture was to be expanded, largely through the supply of inputs to take advantage of new high-yield seeds becoming available for food grains. The rupee was substantially devalued in 1966, and export incentives were adjusted to promote exports. Controls affecting industry were simplified, and greater reliance was placed on the price mechanism to achieve industrial efficiency.

The Fourth Five Year Plan (FY 1969-73) called for a 24 per cent increase over the third plan in real terms of public development expenditures. The public sector accounted for 60 per cent of plan expenditures, and foreign aid contributed 13 per cent of plan financing. Agriculture, including irrigation, received 23 per cent of public outlays; the rest was mostly spent on electric power, industry, and transportation. Although the plan projected national income growth at 5.7 percent a year, the realized rate was only 3.3 percent.

The Fifth Five Year Plan (FY 1974-78) was drafted in late 1973 when crude oil prices were rising rapidly; the rising prices quickly forced a series of revisions. The plan was subsequently approved in late 1976 but was terminated at the end of FY 1977 because a new government wanted different priorities and programmes. The Fifth Plan was in effect only one year, although it provided some guidance to investments throughout the five-year period. The economy operated under annual plans in FY 1978 and FY 1979.

The Sixth Five-Year Plan (FY 1980-84) was intended to be flexible and was based on the principle of annual "rolling" plans. It called for development expenditures of nearly Rs. 1.9 trillion (in FY 1979 prices), of which 90 per cent would be financed from domestic sources, 57 percent of which would come from the public sector. Public-sector development spending would be concentrated in energy (29 per cent); industry including mining (16 per cent); transportation 916 percent); and social services (14 per cent. In practice, slightly more was spent on social services at the expense of transportation and energy. The plan called for GDP growth to increase by 5.1 per cent a year, a target that was surpassed by 0.3 per cent. A major objective of the plan was to increase employment, especially in rural areas, in order to reduce the level of poverty. Poor people were given cows, bullock carts, and handlooms; however, subsequent studies inducted that the income of only about 10 percent of the poor rose above the poverty level.

The Seventh Five Year Plan (FY 1985-89) envisioned a greater emphasis on the allocation of resources to energy and social spending at the expense of industry and agriculture. In practice, the main increase was in transportation and communications, which took up 17 per cent of public-sector expenditure during this period. Total spending was targeted at nearly Rs. 3.9 trillion, of which 94 per cent would be financed from domestic resources, including 48 per cent from the public sector. The planners assumed that public savings would increase and help finance government spending. In practice that increase did not occur; instead, the government relied on foreign borrowing for a greater share of resource that expected.

The schedule for the Eighth Five Year Plan (FY 1992-96) was affected by changes of government and by growing uncertainty over what role planning could usefully perform in a more liberal economy. Two annual plans were in effect in FY 1990 and FY 1991. The eighth plan was finally launched in April 1992 and emphasized market-based policy reform rather than quantitative targets. Total spending was planned at Rs. 8.7 trillion, of which 94 per cent of which would come from domestic resources, 45 per cent of which would come from the public sector.

The eighty plan included three general goals. First, it sought to cut back the public sector by selling off failing and inessential industries while encouraging private investment in such sectors as power, steel, and transport. Second, it proposed that agriculture and rural development have priority. Third, it sought to renew the assault on illiteracy and improve other aspects of social infrastructure, such as the provision of fresh drinking water. Government documents issued in 1992 indicated that GDP growth was expected to increase from around 5 per cent a year during the seventh plan to 5.6 per cent a year during the eighth plan. However, in 1994 economists expected annual growth to be around 4 percent during the period of the eighth plan.

Four decades of planning show that India's economy, a mix of public and private enterprise, is too large and diverse to be wholly predictable or responsive to directions of the planning authorities. Actual results usually differ in important respects from plan targets. Major shortcomings include insufficient improvement in income distribution and alleviation of poverty, delayed completions and cost overruns on many public-sector projects, and far too small a return on many public-sector investments. Even though the plans have turned out to be less effective than expected, they help guide investment priorities, policy recommendations, and financial mobilization.

Rural Indian Infrastructure

Five decades of development planning in India has been unable to ensure a decent living for a large number of people residing in rural areas. Despite many large scale rural development schemes, the absolute number of people in poverty has not declined substantially; abject poverty still remains ubiquitous in rural regions. Lack of or inadequate basic infrastructure, both social and physical, continues to remain a major constraint to progress in numerous villages and their habitations. Even during the last decade of economic reform process, started in 1991, the dismal state of rural infrastructure has hardly improved.

The natural reluctance of private investors in rural infrastructure projects has been based on not only no or low returns to their capital but also uncertainties and delays involved in realizing anticipated revenue from the poverty-stricken users. This shying away syndrome of private capital from rural 'unprofitable' projects has been observed, in this paper, for such critical sectors as sanitation, drinking water, roads and housing. Whereas the role of the state remains crucial in promoting these sectors, an aspect which has been seriously neglected concerns land reforms. The significance of land as a key endowment in rural areas needs to be reconsidered as an important option, which will go a long way increasing effective demand for rural infrastructure and its efficient utilization can be ensured at the grass root level.

Rural infrastructure assumes great importance in India because of the country's predominantly rural nature, the crucial linkages of infrastructure to economic growth, poverty alleviation and human development, and the poor availability of rural infrastructure.

Problems of rural infrastructure provision are different from those of the urban, given the smaller size, density and per capita incomes of rural agglomerations. While privatization is now being considered as the giver of increasing efficiency in the provision of urban infrastructure, this policy recommendation has to be modified in the case of rural infrastructure. Private investors will tend to shun rural areas, especially the ones remote or those that have low incomes or low population density, because of low expected rates of return. It is necessary, therefore, to have a public-private partnership where subsidies or incentives provided by the government would help to direct private investment towards these disadvantaged areas.

At a few cases including the issue of power/electricity

and notes that it might be more efficient to use mini-generators instead of wired networks connected to the main grid. Similarly, in the case of telecom, mobile phone services might be more economical that landlines. Setting up large water treatment plants, modern piped water supply and sewerage networks can also be ruled out. Instead, it may be necessary to have small water treatment plants, water supply through stand posts, and sanitized pit latrines. Several reforms are suggested: industry structure: structural reforms primarily concerned with the introduction of competition into a sector or the removal of barriers to entry so that contestability is a real option

- *Operation:* conduct reforms, whereby a natural monopoly is constrained by rules covering areas such as quality, pricing and access.
- *Ownership:* reforms are often associated with a change in the ownership of previously state-owned enterprises to some form of private sector ownership.
- *Change in regulations:* regulations can often have an adverse impact on welfare, for example, regulations aimed at controlling prices and entry into markets are likely to reduce the average standard of living.

The concept of universal access to infrastructure needs to be changed from time to time. For example, universal access in telecommunications might involve community access at first, followed by institutional access, and then household access. It is opened that this kind of stated introduction of infrastructure will also encourage the generation of local knowledge and debate as to what process of rural development will work best for the individual community.

Primary Health Care and Health Education in Rural India

The objective is to improve and enhance the services offered by Primary Health Centres (PHCs) in the rural communities of India. We propose to do this by applying novel solutions that take advantage of developments in harnessing solar power, computers, and information technology. Our strategy is to use technology to provide effective early medical intervention, deliver expert health care, and minimize the inconvenience caused to patients and health-workers from poor logistics and long travel time. An equally important role of PHCs is to provide health education emphasizing family planning, hygiene, sanitation, and prevention of communicable diseases. A final step in this process will happen through video consulting and examination, a technology we anticipate becoming available in rural areas by year 2010.

Overview

The long-term goal of the Indian government and international funding agencies has been to provide health care to rural communities through PHCs. However, even with large funding, these centres have not been successful for a variety of reasons that include lack of decent facilities, equipment for performing even simple laboratory tests, etc. Even more important is a social reality: the just are not enough trained and qualified doctors to adequately serve the entire urban and rural populations of India even if we could provide financial incentives for them to work in rural areas. Since we believe that the dearth of doctors willing to practice in rural areas and their reluctance to travel to, let alone live in, remote areas will continue to exist fro a long time to come, we have incorporated this reality into our planning from the start as described in this proposal. Our plan, therefore, is to increase the effectiveness of doctors who are willing to work in rural areas by a large factor. This can be accomplished by reducing the need for doctors in the initial screening of patients, and by allocating one physician for every five PHCs. Simultaneously; we plan to make working at PHCs more attractive and satisfying.

The result of non-functioning PHCs has been that, in many cases diseases are not diagnosed in their early stages nor treated. The rural population has to often travel to urban areas when they can no longer bear the suffering caused by the disease, thus increasing the load on hospitals in urban areas and ending up with serious complication that, in many cases, could have easily been treated at their early stages. The need to rectify this problem has become critical especially given the fact that over 650 million people live in rural areas across the country with poor awareness of health issues. This ignorance, coupled with the increased mobility between rural and urban areas, has led to an explosive increase in the spread of diseases like HIV/AID and Hepatitis B and C.

We envisage PHCs functioning as the first level in a hierarchical system of health care facilities. At this primary level, PHCs will play two equally important roles: First, diagnosis of diseases based on symptoms and simple laboratory tests, and their treatment either at the centres or through referral. Second, health education leading to family planning, better hygiene and sanitation, and prevention of communicable diseases, especially sexually transmitted diseases.

The government has shown keep interest in finding private partners to revitalize the PHCs. To this end The George Foundation, in collaboration with the Government of Tamil Nadu, has initiated a pilot project involving one PHC covering some 79,000 people in the Dharamapuri District. Five more PHCs will soon be included in the pilot project. The goal is to build on the existing "infrastructure" at these PHCs, make them functional and enhance their capability. The George Foundation will coordinate and manage this proposed project.

Enhancing the Capabilities of the PHC

The first step is to furbish the existing PHCs (land, building, equipment, and supplies) already set up by the government. We anticipate each PHC to consist of an initial screening room with a computer, an examination room for the doctor, a laboratory for medical tests and supplies, and toilets. The furnishing will be simple, comfortable, and durable.

The most critical infrastructure element is electricity. We propose to use either solar panels or diesel generators (depending on a cost-benefit analysis) connected to batteries for uninterrupted electric power for computers and laboratory equipment. Such unites have already been field tested by The George Foundation at its boarding school for economically disadvantaged children, Shanti Bhawan, and will assure the operation of equipment for much of the day even when conventional electric power is unavailable.

Each PHC will have a full time staff consisting of a paramedic individual to perform initial screening with the computer, a trained nurse or physicians' assistant, and a laboratory technician. We anticipate that a qualified medical doctor will be shared between 3-5 PHCs in a given area. Training of this staff in the novel technology and in the holistic approach we are proposing will be extensive and continuous, and their performance will be monitored constantly as described in Appendices B and C.

In addition to the testing capability of the on-site medical laboratory, a crucial tool for diagnosis will be the computer. A software programme called EDPS2000 shall assist the technician in maintaining, in a protected and confidential manner, the medical history of all patients, in suggesting tests to perform, and to evaluate possible causes based on the symptoms displayed or the description given by the patient. It will also incorporate the medical history in making the probable diagnosis. In addition, based on this diagnosis, it will also prescribe medicines for minor illnesses, which will be sold at cost by the PHC. In cases of probable major illnesses or when the diagnosis is not clear, the computer output will propose a future course of action-further tests and possibly a visit to a specialist. In the latter case, the computer will print out the patient's relevant/essential history that can be taken to the specialist. We anticipate that the majority of cases will be handled at the level of PHCs, thus drastically cutting down the burden placed on hospitals and doctors.

Patients visiting PHCs will also be provided health education by the staff through posters and through audiovisual demonstrations. Providing information and help with family planning, and awareness on communicable diseases, will be a key role of the staff. Community programmes for which we shall form collaborations with Non-Governmental agencies (NGOs) and social workers will supplement these activities.

At present we envisage each PHC to be an isolated unit. All software updates and sharing of information would have to be uploaded/downloaded periodically by a person travelling from centre to centre. We plan to connect each PHC to its assigned doctor through wireless communication and a palm computer. Over a three-year time frame we propose to connect the computers at different PHCs through standard telephone and/or cell phone link to a central coordination/support centre. The central facility will then be able to collect and update the data from all PHCs within its jurisdiction, and perform pattern detection and epidemiological analysis, thereby predicting epidemics and exposing widespread health problems in their early stages. In addition to simplifying the uploading/ downloading of data onto the central computer, this enhancement will allow on-line access to specialists via e-mail, further reducing patient's travel time and cost and the load on urban health care facilities.

As a final step, we anticipate enhancing the diagnostic capability of PHCs through video consultations wherein the patient (through the PHC) will access a physician (and even a anticipate that this technology and the required transmission rate using cellular connections will become a reality in rural India in 5-10 years.

Health Education and Disease Prevention

Rural India faces many very serious problems. Notable amongst them are potable water, emerging pandemics, population control, good hygiene and sanitation practices, basic education, and simple techniques for improving their crops and lives. One cannot expect to upgrade the people's health without simultaneously making an impact on these issues, and vice versa. We will, therefore, train and empower the staff at the PHCs to spread awareness on some of these issues, build trust within the community, ad to take a holistic approach to health care.

Using the telephone link to the central facility, relevant training and educational material and specific health instructions will be periodically transmitted to the computers at all PHCs, and the status of various educational programmes will be monitored.

Community Involvement

For the PHCs to be effective, people have to believe that the PHCs are there to server them and to provide value. To facilitate this we plan to involve the local population in the operation and in the community outreach programmes. We also plan to encourage cultural activities, self-help programmes, and health education through the PHCs. The George Foundation will be to evaluate the performance of PHCs and to provide guidance. Evaluation will be based on one simple criterion—whether the PHCs have significantly improved the health and well being of the community.

Description of EDPS 2000

The Early Detection & Prevention System (EDPS 2000) is a software system developed by Dr. Abraham George, the founder of The George Foundation, a non-profit trust. It can provide early diagnosis of patient's health status. EDPS2000 screens patients and identifies those who need prompt attention by qualified physicians, while recommending treatment for others with minor illnesses.

It provides a probable diagnosis of disease conditions based on the complaints narrated by the patient along with the results of a few relevant laboratory test and the patient's medical history. It must be understood that this software does not aim to give a confirmatory diagnosis in most cases, but only a probable diagnosis. Several conditions are supported by laboratory tests, which in turn, may enable the user to make a confirmatory diagnosis. It should, therefore, be seen only as a first line of intervention whereby the patient, equipped with a probable diagnosis, can then go on to the next level, like referral to a specialist, then required. Several minor or common illnesses will be treated at this level on instructions given by the software.

As of now, the diseases covered by EDPS 2000 are based on the common disease patterns seen in South India. This list of approximately 300 diseases is presented. A special team from both India and the United States has designed this software over the past two years, and The George Foundation has exclusive license to use in selected areas in rural India. The system is being maintained ad enhanced under license by eMedexOnline LLC, a U.S. based company. It has been extensively tested with over 10,000 patients in three leading hospitals in Bangalore for accuracy and acceptance by both the user and the patient.

Another aspect of the EDPS software is maintaining a database of doctors and hospital/clinics to whom referrals are made. By prior arrangements made by The George

Foundation with doctors and hospitals/clinics, we hope to cut down on the cost and hardship incurred by the patients.

Electricity and Water Revolution in Rural Areas

There are two major crises affecting rural areas of India—lack of electricity and clean drinking water. Shortage of electricity directly hampers rural economic growth while non-availability of clean drinking water does it indirectly by creating tremendous health problems. Both these problems can be solved simultaneously by village-level power plants running on locally produced renewable fuels like biogas, biodiesel, ethanol and pyrolysis oil.

Their internal combustion power plants, like diesel gensets, of 500 kW capacity each can supply enough electricity for an average village with a population of 2000-3000 people. In addition, the high temperature exhaust gases from these plants can easily distill or boil water via a suitably designed unit, which can be attached to the genset. Hence the 500 kW power plant can produce about 150,000 litres of clean drinking water every day. Thus the power plant will produce both electricity and water simultaneously. The raw water could be from any source like river, canal, rainwater harvesting tanks or shallow wells.

In producing both electricity and clean water the power plant efficiency will jump from existing 35% to around 65% thereby making the whole system extremely efficient. Most of the energy of these gensets is lost in exhaust gases and in cooling the engine. This energy can easily be utilized for distillation or water boiling.

The plant can be owned by a microutility company whose shares will be owned by all the villagers. It can therefore be managed professionally and hence will not have the pitfalls of a cooperative society, which very rapidly degenerates, into political chaos. Another interesting feature of this microutility could be that it will lease the village level transmission lines and infrastructure from the local State Electricity Boards (SEBs) at "social cost". This can be based on the cost of electricity that most of the SEBs charge farmers presently. The village thus could be isolated from the SEB network and appropriate meters installed so that SEB electricity could be metered. During the maintenance schedule of microutility it could draw upon the SEB's electricity. With the new electricity Act (2003) it is possible for microutilities to do so. Thus the microutility will sell electricity and clean drinking water to the village. For agriculture and other non-drinking purposes the villages can take water from any other source.

The renewable fuel for running these gensets can be biogas, biodiesel, ethanol or pyrolysis oil.

Biogas, which is, produced either from cowdung or any biomass has been used for almost 100 years in India as a cooking fuel. However it can easily be used to run diesel gensets. It is envisaged that the microutility will buy the biomass residues from the villages and use them in a sophisticated digester to produce biogas efficiently. Some development is still needed in engineering the digesters so that they can run very efficiently and on varied biomass. Biogas production from these digesters improves drastically if the temperature, pH and other variables are maintained properly. This requires sophisticated controls, which a microutility can easily install.

Biodiesel is another fuel, which can be used in the diesel gensets directly. It is produced from non-edible oils like Karanja, Neem or Jatropha.

There is national technology mission on biodiesel and large-scale plantations of some of these crops are planned. However for it to become a viable alternative to diesel it is necessary that the present crop yields are increased manifold, so that farmers get excellent remuneration from growing them. At present, in the absence of any large-scale plantations this is still a paper exercise showing overblown economic benefits. Hence there is a need to have a national programme for breeding and selecting high yielding varieties of non-edible oilseed-bearing crops.

Ethanol traditionally has been produced from sugary crops like sugarcane. In India it is mostly produced from molasses, which is a by-product of sugar industry. However, with 5% ethanol mix in petrol promoted by Government of India for automotive uses, the present ethanol production needs to be increased manifold. There is therefore a need to use other crops which require less inputs than sugarcane and are short duration crops.

Sweet sorghum is such a crop. It is a multipurpose crop, which produces grain, sweet juice from its stem ad the bagasse is excellent as cattle feed. Besides it uses almost 50% less water than sugarcane and is a 4-month crop so farmers can grow two crops/year on the same land. Nimbkar Agricultural Research Institute (NARI) has pioneered the development of sweet sorghum in India since 1970s. NARI has produced a high yielding sweet sorghum hybrid 'Madhura'. Thus "Madhura" planted on the same area where grain or fodder sorghum is grown presently in the country can yield simultaneously about 2000 million litres of ethanol and 10 million tones of grain every year.

Similarly spoiled grain which cannot be used for human or cattle consumption can also be used for ethanol production via the starch hydrolysis route. Recently US and European scientists have reported a breakthrough in technology for using any agricultural residues for ethanol production. This can help increase further the ethanol production from biomass. Ethanol fuel of 85% and above concentration can be used in any spark ignition engine and hence these gensets can run on ethanol produced easily from existing distilleries. Thus there is no need to produce costly 100% anhydrous ethanol which is required for mixing in petrol. This can help reduce the cost of electricity form these utilities.

Pyrolysis oil is similar to diesel and can be used in the diesel gensets directly. It is produced by rapid combustion of dry agricultural residues. India produces more than 400 million tonnes of agricultural residues every year. Thus there is a potential of producing from these residues pyrolysis oil equivalent to 86 million tonnes of diesel every year. This is nearly 60% of total oil demand of the country. This oil has been successfully tested in 5 MW diesel gensets in Europe. Small-scale pyrolysis oil production units in rural areas can be run quite effectively.

It is estimated that renewable liquid and gaseous fuel production and usage in rural areas could be Rs. 20-3,000-crore/year industry ($4.5-6.5 billion) and can bring substantial wealth to these areas. Besides it will bring energy and water self-sufficiency to village.

For these plants to be introduced on large scale in villages it is necessary to set up a National mission on electricity and water production for rural areas. This mission may provide grants for developing such plants, help in setting up the microutilities by providing them financial help and should encourage the government, corporate sector and NGO partnership in this vital area.

Development of dual-purpose power plants may also help in disaster relief management. During most of the disasters like earthquake and Tsunami type flooding, electricity and clean drinking water are in short supply. These power plants of 250-500 kW capacities can easily be truck mounted and can be sent to the disaster areas. Their large-scale usage in rural areas will allow the availability of such plants for disaster relief on a short notice.

Schooling in Rural India

About one third of all Indian children are out of school. In the large north Indian states, which account for over 40% of the country's population, the proportion of out-of-school children in the 6-14 age group is as high as 41% rising to 54% among female children.

Considering the crucial role of elementary education in development, the universalisation of schooling in India is one of the most urgent development issues in the world today. Yet, relatively little is known about the precise reasons why so many Indian children are out of school. In public debates, the tendency is to highlight a single 'explanation'. In official circles, for instance, the problem is often blamed on parental indifference towards education—a convenient argument since it diverts attention from the responsibility of the state. Others consider that child labour is the overwhelming obstacle: according to the Campaign Against Child Labour (1997), India has more than 60 million child labourers, working 12 hours a day on average. Neither of these single-focus explanations, however, stands up to careful scrutiny. This is not to deny that they contain a grain of truth. The real challenge is to build a balanced picture of the determinants of school participation, which integrates different lines of explanations: lock of parental or child motivation, the costs of schooling, the demands of child labour, and the low quality of schooling, among others.

As a modest step in that direction, this paper presents an analysis of the determinants of school participation based on a recent survey of schooling in north India, the PROBE survey.

The PROBE survey, however, offers unusual possibilities for scrutinizing different influences on schooling decisions, in so far as it contains detailed information not only on the characteristics of about 4,400 children and their households, but also on the schools to which these children have access. In particular, this survey enables us to examine the influence of different types of 'school quality' variables on school participation and educational achievements in rural India.

The Schooling Situation in Rural India

By way of orientation, we begin with a brief sketch of the schooling situation in rural India, with specific reference to the four major states covered by the PROBE survey: Bihar, Madhya Pradesh, Rajasthan, Uttar Pradesh (hereafter the 'PROBE states').

The main features of the schooling situation in these states, as they emerge from the PROBE survey, include the following

School availability: Most villages have at least one government primary school (classes 1 to 5). Government schools charge negligible fees, and never refuse to enroll a child. There are no Board examination until class 5 (in fact, well after class 5 in most states), but primary schools conduct school tests and children are sometimes asked to repeat a particular class. Only a minority of village—about 30%—have a 'middle' school (classes 6 to 8).

Private schools: In addition to government schools, private schools with primary sections are available in a significant minority (about 17%) of villages. Private schools charge fees, and generally attract children from relatively privileged families, though children from poor families are not entirely excluded.

Parental motivation: Qualitative data from the PROBE survey suggest that parental interest in education is generally quite high. Most parents would like their children (particularly sons) to be educated, and favour compulsory education for all children, however, they have a dim view of the schooling system, and endless complaints about teaching standards in government schools.

School participation: In the 6-14 age group, according to the PROBE survey, 85% of boys and 56% of girls are currently enrolled in school.

Among ever-enrolled children in the 13-18 age group, 81% have completed class 5.

Child labour: Time utilization data from the PROBE survey indicate that out-of-school children work about 4.7 hours a day on average (about 2 hours more than school-going children), mainly helping their parents at home and in the fields. Work hours are a little longer for girls than for boys, and particularly long for eldest daughters in poor families.

School quality: Aside from parental testimonies, the PROBE survey found much direct evidence of the dismal state of government schools. To illustrate: *(1)* Only one fourth of the sample schools have at least tow teachers, two all-weather classrooms, and some teaching aids; *(2)* If all children aged 6-10 in the sample villages were enrolled in a government primary school, there would be more than 100 pupils per classroom on average, and 68 pupils for each teacher; *(3)* At the time of the investigators' visit, about half of the schools had no teaching activity.

Silver lining: Aside from the four major states listed earlier, the PROBE survey also covered Himachal Pradesh, a smaller state located in the Himalayan region. In sharp contrast with the other states, Himachal Pradesh had high rates of school participation (96% of all children aged 6-14 were studying), and low educational disparities between boys and girls as well as between different communities. There were also many signs of a higher quality of schooling in Himachal Pradesh, e.g. lower pupil-teacher ratios, better teaching standards, and a more cooperative rapport between parents and teachers. This success is all the more impressive considering that, not so long ago, Himachal Pradesh was widely regarded as a 'backward' region of north India.

3

Rural Marketing Strategies in India

Marketing channels are routes through which agricultural products move from producers to consumers. The length of the channel varies from commodity to commodity, depends on the quality to be moved, the form of consumer demand and degree of regional specialization in production. The chain of intermediaries through whom the various food grains pass producers to consumers constitutes their marketing channels and also as alternative routes of product flows from producers to consumers.

Factors Affecting Length of Marketing Channels

Marketing channels for a agriculture products vary from product to product, country to country, lot to lot and time to time. For example, the marketing channels for fruits are different form those for good grains. Packagers play a crucial role in the marketing in fruits. The level of the development of a society or country determines the final form in which consumers demand the product. For example, consumers in developed countries demand more processed foods in a packed form. Wheat has to be supplied in the form of bread. Most eatables have to be cooked and packed properly before they reach the consumers. Processors play a dominant role in such societies. In developing countries like India, however most food grains are purchased by consumers in the raw form and processing is done at the consumer's level. Again the lots of originating at small farms follow different route channels from the one originating in large farms. For example, small farms usually sell their produce to village traders; it may or may not enter the main market. But large farms usually sell their produce in the main market, where it goes into the hands of wholesalers. The produce sold immediately after the harvest usually follows longer channel than the one sold in later months.

With the expansions in transportations and communications network changes in the structure of demand and development of markets, marketing. Channel for farm products in India have undergone a considerable charge, both in terms of length and quality.

Marketing Channels for Food Grains

Marketing channels for various cereals in India are more or less similar except the channel for paddy (or rice) where rice millers come into the picture. For pulse crops, dal mills appear prominently in the channel. The flow chart enables us to know the marketing channels for general food grains in India.

Some common marketing channels for Food grains have been identified as follows:

- Farmer to consumers
- Farmer to retailer or village trader to consumer
- Farmer to wholesaler to retailer to consumer
- Farmer to village trader to wholesaler to retailer to consumer

- Farmer to co–operative marketing society to retailer to consumer
- Farmer to a government agency (FCI etc) to Fair Price shop-owner to consumer.
- Farmer to wholesaler to flour miller to retailer to consume.

The channels for paddy-rice and pulses are broadly the same; expect that the rice millers of dal millers come in to the picture before the produce reaches retailers of consumers.

Marketing Channels for Oil Seeds

Marketing channels for oilseeds are different from those for food grains mainly because the extractions of oil from oilseeds is an important marketing functions of oil seeds.

The most common marketing channels for oilseeds in India are:

(i) Producer to consumer (who either directly consumes the oilseeds or gets it processed on customer basis)

(ii) Producer to village trader to oil retailer to consumer

(iii) Producer to oilseed wholesaler to processor to oil wholesaler to oil retailer to oil consumers

(iv) Producer to village trader to oil consumers

(v) Producer to government agency to processor to oil wholesaler to oil retailer to oil consumer.

Rural Marketing in India

A silent revolutions in sweeping the India's countryside. It has compelled marketing whizkids to rural areas. The marketing battle field has shifted from the cities to the villages "Go rural" seems to be the latest slogan. The rural consumer is discerning and the rural market is vibrant. At the current rate of growth it will soon out step the urban market. The rural market is not sleeping any longer. Today the India's rural market is regarded as the bigger hope of demand recovery. Marketers and manufactures have realized the burgeoning, purchasing power, vast size and demand base of the once neglected hinterland. Now efforts are as to accentuate the attitude of the rural consumers. The marketing move of many companies being tailored to rural tastes and lifestyles. The indigenous companies are not only concentrating there marketing activates, but MNC's also have or cached in remote rural areas at present. The government policies, development of information technology, corporate strategies and satellite communications are the factors responsible for the developed rural marketing. The India's rural market with its vast size and demand base offers great opportunities to the marketers. Nearly three fourth of the country's consumers are in the rural market and half the national income is generated there.

Population of India

Area	*1991 population (in crore)*	*% Total*	*2000 population (in crore)*	*% Total*
Rural	64.1	76	74	73
Urban	20.3	24	29	27
Total	84.4		100	100

Sources: Census of India.

The term 'Rural Marketing' which was earlier used as an umbrella term to refer all commercial transactions of rural people, acquired a separate meaning of great significance in 1990's.

Percentage Distribution of Households, Population and Income

	House Holds	Population	Income
Rural	72.6	74.6	55.6
Urban	27.4	25.4	44.4
All India	100.0	100.0	100.0

Source: MIMAD – Micro Impact of Macro and Adjustment Policies.

The rural consumer is discerning and the rural market is vibrant. At the current rate of growth it will soon out strip the urban market. The changing times clearly necessitate an over al of marketing strategies for marketing wanting to benefit from rising rural consumerism.

Rural market refused to marketing of rural products in rural and urban areas and agricultural inputs in rural markets. It was considered synonymous to 'Agricultural Marketing'

Phase I (Before Mid–1960's)

From / To	*Rural*	*Urban*
Urban	Agricultural inputs – consumables	Not relevant
Rural	Artisan Services and Products	Agriculture Produce

Green revolutions ushered in scientific farming practices and transferred many of the poor villages into prosperous busy centres. As a result the demand for agricultural inputs went up. Better irrigation facilities soil, testing, use of high yield variety seeds, fertilizers pesticides and employment of machinery like power tillers, harvesters, threshers etc., changed the rural scenario.

Phase II (1960s–1990s)

From/To	*Rural*	*Urban*
Urban	Agricultural inputs - consumables	Not relevant
Rural	Artisan Services and Products	Agriculture Produce

What was not considered so far during the low earlier phases was that of marketing of house holds. Consumables and durables to the rural markets. First there was no rural market as such. The existing rural markets for these products were not substantial—not large to attract the attention of the urban marketers.

Secondly they were in accessible. The small villages/ hamlets were widely scattered marketing reach difficult and expensive. The economic reforms of 1991-1992 further accelerated the process by introducing competition in the rural markets. Steadily, the rural markets has grown for house hold consumable and durables.

Phase III—After 1990s

From/to	*Rural*
Urban	Occupational inputs: Consumables and durables House hold goods consumables and durables
Rural	Artisan services and products

Rural Work and Earnings

S.No	*Aspects*	*Male*	*Female*
1	Average no of days worked	327	246
2	Average daily earnings (Rs) (casual labour)	28.27	18.27
3	Earning Per worker (Rs)	9234	4494
4	Earnings Per Capita (Rs)	4903	1344
5	Rate of growth of earnings per worker (%)	3.41	3.52
6	Rate of growth of earnings per Capita (%)	2.71	1.92

Rural Market Demographics

S.No	Aspect	Male	Female	Total
1	Population ('000)	367,240	344,640	711,880
2	Work for ('000)	271,370	1,21,820	393,190
3	Student Population ratio (per 1000)	707	631	
	age-wise	777	635	
	5-9	413	259	
	10-14	86	29	
	15-19			
	20-24			
4	Worker population ratio (per 1000)			
	age-wise	6	7	
	5-9	91	96	
	10-14	503	304	
	15-19	844	409	
	20-24	970	550	
	25-59	639	218	
	60+	531	299	
	All ages			
5	Un employment rates for educated	69	204	
	(per 1000) secondary Graduate+	107	351	
6	Occupational distribution (per 1000)	531		
	Agriculture, forestry and fishery	7	3	
	Mining and quarrying	115	102	
	Manufacturing and repair services	4	0.3	
	Electricity, gas and water	57	17	
	Constructions	131	43	
	Trade, hotels and restaurants	52	4	
	Transport, storage and communication	16	4	
	Finance, insurance, real estate and business services Community solid and personal services	87	79	

Per Capita House-Hold Expenditure (in Rupees)

Level	*States*	*Expenditure*
High (above Rs 382)	Punjab	614
	Kerala	604
	Haryana	546
	Rajasthan	452
	Gujarat	416
	Andhra Pradesh	386
	Maharashtra	384
Average (Rs. 382)	West Bengal	382
	Orissa	381
	Tamilnadu	381
	Uttar Pradesh	373
	Karnataka	365
Low (Below Rs. 350)	Assam	338
	Madhya Pradesh	326
	Bihar	289

Source: National Sample survey (Jan.-June) 1990 facts for your 2000.

Consumer Durables: Rural Vs Urban

Groups	*Areas*	*Million units*		*Growth of Charge*		*Over precious period*
		1994-95	*2001-02*	*2001-02*	*2006-07*	*2006-07*
I	Urban	140.10	195.15	245.09	39.29	25.29
	Rural	224.17	330.63	430.93	47.49	30.34
II	Urban	61.44	95.54	122.70	55.50	28.42
	Rural	43.54	100.13	144.83	129.97	44.64
III	Urban	35.99	83.05	138.31	130.76	66.54
	Rural	11.24	29.90	57.10	166.01	90.97

Rural FMCG Market Projections

Category	*Growth%*	*2001-02* *Total Share*	*Rural*	*2006* *Total Share*	*Rural*	*Rural Market share*
Toilet Soap	13.4	9645	6021	18086	11291	62.4
Body talc/ powder	23.65	1445	793	4327	2292	54.1
Tooth paste	23.50	3198	1441	9376	4140	45.1
Cooking Medium/ vanspati	7.63	4549	2846	6648	4108	62.6
Tea	10.97	8009	4955	13495	8337	61.9
Health Beverages	28.54	.60	5398	2110	39.8	39.8
Electric Bulbs	9.40	354	1371	555	31.7	31.7
Electric tubes	10.15	.74	308	121	38.7	38.7
Cigarettes	13.09	9784	6422	18026	11879	65.6
Packaged Biscuits	6.79	2862	1322	4014	1837	46.2
Hair oil/ cream	30.85	300	179	1159	689	59.7
Cooking medicine oil	1091	20946	15,731	35,295	25806	73.4

Source: Business Intelligence Unit and NCAER *Business World,* 11 October 1989.

Sales Potentials of Haats and Melas

Number of Haats	47000
Average per day sales in haats	2,23,000
Average outlets per haat	314
Average visitors to a haat	4,580 (covers five villages)
Average sales per outlet in haat	Rs. 874
Purchase of Manufacture goods in a haat	24.3 percent
Number of Commercial melas	5000
Sales Per day in mela	Rs. 25 lakh

Source: Pradeep Kashyap, MART quoted in A & M February 1999.

Sales Potential of HAATS and MELAS

Aspect	*West*	*North*	*South*	*East*	*Total*
Village with less than 5000 people	2,00,106	73,585	1,61,982	1,35,936	4,35,673
Villages with pucca resorts	78,217	43,102	41,348	44,693	2,07,360
Village with number of outlets	9,75,911	9,80,728	10,89,603	6,51,285	32,53,602
Villages with number of haats	11,436	3167	18905	8389	41,897

Source: Business World, 11 October 1999.

Top 100 Melas of India

State	*Mela/Fair*	*Location*	*District*	*Month*	*Duration*	*Visitors (In Lakhs)*
Assam	Raasmela	Bilasipura	Dhubri	Nov	30	0.5
	Netaji mela	Karimgunj	Karim gunj	Jan	15	0.7
	Rash mahotsav	Harimandir	Nalbari	Nov	11	1.0
Andhra Pradesh	Brahmo-stavam	Tirupathi	Chittoor	Sep/Oct.	10	10 lakhs
	Pyditthal-Imma Utsavam	Vijayana-garam	Vijayana-garam	April/May	7	2 lakhs
	Sivarathri mela	Kalahasti	Chittoor	Feb	4	1 lakhs
BIHAR	Sonepur mela	Sonepur	Patna	Nov	30	1 lakhs
	Sorath mela	Sorath	Madhu-bani	June	15	10 lakhs
	Vaisakh purnima	Bodhgaya	Gaya	April/May	15	2 lakhs
	Shivarathri mela	Sayal	Hazari-bagh	Feb.	15	0.7 lakhs

GUJARAT	Vautha fair	Vautha	Ahmed-abad	Nov	6	10 lakhs
	Somnath fair	Patan	Junagarh	Nov	4	1 lakhs
	Narsingaji fair	Gomipur	Ahemed-abad	Nov	1	2 lakhs
	Bhavnath fair	Junagarh	Junagarh	Feb	1	0.7 lakhs
	Navarathri fair	Ambhaji	Banas-kantha	Sept	10	0.8 lakhs
	Lillipuri Kram fair	Junagarh	Junagarh	Nov	5	1 lakhs
	Manekthari Poonam fair	Dakor	Kheda	Sept	1	1.5 lakhs
	Gadhadar fair	Shyamlaji	Sabar-kantha	Nov	7	1 lakhs
	Gokulash-tami fair	Surat	Surat	Aug	7	1 lakhs
HARYANA	Pihowa mela	Pihowa	Kuruk-shetra	Mar	30	5 lakhs
	Pathrimata ka mela	Pathri	Panipat	Mar/July	30	5 lakhs
	Ganjor mela	Sirsa	Sirsa	April	3	1 lakh
	Kapal-mochan mela	Bilaspur	Yamuna-nagar	Nov	5	2 lakhs
	Surajkund mela	Faridabad	Farida-bad	Feb		
	Kisan mela	Karnal	Karnal	Sep	9	2 lakhs
	Dehja mela	Ladana	Kaithal	Oct	7	1 lakhs
KERALA	Pooram festival	Trichur	Trichur	April	21	7 Lakhs
	Onam	Trivendrum	Triven.	Aug	10	10 Lakhs
	Makara vilakku	Malappuram	Malapp.	Mar	7	10 Lakhs
	Chirappu Feast of Sebastian	Kottayam	Kottayam	Nov/Dec	5	2 Lakhs

	Shivarathri	Chertala	Ernakulam	Jan	7	4 Lakhs
	Vilakku	Aluva	"	Feb/Mar	4	5 Lakhs
	Omallor fair	Omallor	"	Mar	7	4 Lakhs
	Magara	Sabarimala	Idukki	Jan	10	2 Lakhs
	Jyothi	Kannur	Kannur	April	5	2 Lakhs
	Sri Sundareshwar utsavam	Vadakkara	Mallap.	Mar.	3	10 Lakhs
MP	Kartikmela	Ujjain	Ujjain	Nov	30	20 Lakhs
	Kadam mela	Kharagpur	Tikamgarh	Nov	15	0.6 Lakhs
	Gwalior trade fair	Gwalior	Gwalior	Jan	30	10 Lakhs
	Makara Sankrathi	Baraman	Ujjain	Jan	30	10 Lakhs
PUNJAB	Rural Olympics	Quila Raipur	Ludhiana	Jan/Feb	7	3 Lakhs
	Hollah mohalla	Anandpur sahib	Ropar	Mar	5	3 Lakhs
	Baisakhi	Talwandi Sahib	Bhatinda	April	5	3 Lakhs
	Sodal-mela	Jalandhar	Jalandhar	Sep	2	8 Lakhs
	Mag-mela	Muktsar	Faridkot	Jan	3	5 Lakhs
	Ramteerth mela	Kaler purnima	Amritsar	Nov	5	1.5 Lakhs
	Sahidijod mela	Fatehgarh Sahib	Patiala	Jan/Feb	4	4 Lakhs
	Chappar mela	Chappar	Ludhiana	Sep	5	3 Lakhs

4

Rural-Urban Divide in India

Rural-urban disparities, particularly in post-colonial countries, have for long been one of the causes of concern for the policy-makers. The disparities are seen in all spheres of human life—economic and non-economic. The extent of disparities, however, differs from country to country. The long colonial rule in India had created an urban-rural divide. What causes great concern now-a-days is the sharp increase in the level of disparities after a few decades of planning, especially because planning was conceived as an instrument to narrow down rural-urban disparities.

Rural India encompasses a little less than three-fourths of the country's population and is characterized by low income levels; poor quality of life and a weak base of human development. Nearly one-third of the national income comes from village, but there is a significant rural-urban divide.

Agriculture is the mainstay of most post-colonial countries. It supports roughly two-thirds of the workforce. But the lion's share of India's national resources is directed to the non-agricultural sector.

The agricultural sector has been growing at less than half the pace of the other sectors. During the Seventh Plan, agriculture and allied sectors grew at a rate of 3.4 per cent, while the national economy grew at 6 per cent. In 1997-98, there was a negative growth of 2 per cent in the agricultural sector, although the national economy grew by 5 per cent.

The slower rate of growth of agriculture has serious implications for the rural-urban relationship. In an article in Alternative Economic Survey, Kripa Shankar has shown that it results in the further widening of the divide, as the following data relating to agricultural and non-agricultural gross domestic product (GDP) at 1980-81 prices indicate. The GDP per agricultural worker was Rs. 2,442.49 in 1950-51, followed by Rs.3,196 in 1970-71 and Rs. 3,627 in 1995-96. The GDP per non-agricultural worker rose sharply from Rs. 4,469.63 in 1950-51 to Rs. 9,179 in 1970-71 and to Rs. 16,715.08 in 1995-96. There has been a further step rise after the Central government accepted the Structural Adjustment Programme. While the GDP per agricultural worker rose from Rs. 3,544.98 in 1990-91 from Rs. 14,660 to Rs. 16,715.08 during same period. The data tend to show that the ratio between the agricultural output per farm worker and the average output per non-farm worker, which was 1:1.83 in 1950-51, rose to 1:4.6 in 1995-96.

The introduction of the policy of liberalization has affected non-farm employment in rural areas. In 1997-98, the annual increase in non-farm employment in rural areas was 4.06 per cent. In 1983-84 it was 3.28 per cent. During 1999-2000 it came down to 2.14 per cent. The consequence has been a very slow reduction in rural poverty. In 1993-94 it was 39.36 per cent, in 1999-2000 the figure came down marginally to 36.35 per cent.

Agricultural investments account for 10 per cent of the total investments in the country. The neglect of agriculture and allied sectors is evident from the budgetary allocation. It has never been more than 20 per cent. In 1997-98 the Central and State governments spent Rs. 12,000 crores on the police, which was marginally lower than the Central and State plan outlay on agriculture and allied actives.

According to one estimate, the average income of an urban dweller is four times higher than that of a rural dweller. Rural deprivation becomes crystal clear if we look at the data on rural India's contribution is 27 per cent but the return is 5 per cent.

The Human Development Report of India (1999) attempted to divide the rural and urban household on the basis of their incomes. The income status is reflected in the per capita consumption expenditure. In 1999-2000 the per capita per month consumption expenditure on the rural areas was Rs. 486.08 and in the case of urban areas it was Rs. 854.96, according to HDR 2002.

Data collected by the National Sample Survey Organisation (NSSO) show that the average per capita expenditure (MPCE) in rural India during 2000-01 amounted to Rs. 914.57 for an urban dweller. Interestingly, the gap between the average for urban and rural areas has widened by over 8 percentage points between 1987-88 and 2000-01. As 1987-88 was a drought year, the increase in the disparity level is all the more significant. The NSSO data so that while 75 per cent of the country's population in 2000-01 resided in rural areas, they accounted for less than 62 per cent of the total consumption expenditure.

If we look at the poverty data, a similar situation is noticed. India, a developing economy of over a billion people, recorded a relatively high economic growth during 1980-2000, especially during the 1990s, a decade known for noteworthy structural economic reforms. This period also recorded a decline in the incidence of poverty and improvement in parameters of human development such as levels of literacy, health and nutrition conditions. Development policies focused on enhanced and targeted public investments in programmes that facilitated improvements in the quality of life of the masses, but the disparity remains.

The disparities in the social development sector are mind-boggling. Rural adult illiteracy is a matter of alarming concern. In 2001, the urban literacy rate was 80.06 per cent but the rural literacy rate was 59.91 per cent. Thus, the difference in rural-urban areas in terms of percentage points is 20.85. Data released by the Planning Commission show that among illiterate people aged 60 years and above, 7.2 per cent live in rural areas. In urban areas the figure is 48.2 per cent. Of the illiterate people who are 15 years and above but not beyond 60 years, rural areas have 55.8 per cent and the urban areas 25.1 per cent.

Of the school-going children in the age group of 5-14 years, 82.4 per cent live in urban areas. The rural figure is 63.3 per cent. Kerala has been able to bring this disparity down quite considerably—71.8 years in rural and 79.8 years in urban areas.

The disparity is noticeable even in respect of the sex ratio. Census 2001 data have shown a general improvement in this regard because in 1991 the sex ration was 927 women for 1,000 men while in 2001 it was 933 women for 1,000 men. The Census data have also given the urban-rural break-up, which shows that while in the case of urban India the ratio is 901 women to 1,000 men, in the case of rural India it is 946 women to 1,000 men.

The Indian state has the primary responsibility to supply safe drinking water to all the people in the country irrespective of their place of habitat. But the situation is far from desirable. The National Sample Survey (NSS) data (1998, 5th round) show that while 70.1 per cent of urban dwellers have access to piped water, in the case of the rural people it is as low as 18.7 per cent. Public health facilities are so inadequate in rural areas that the death rate per 1,000 is 9.6 per cent while in urban areas it is 6 per cent. In rural areas the infant mortality rate is 77 per

1,000 but in urban areas it is al low as 45.

Data on rural–urban disparity on the availability of sanitary facilities indicate the gravity of the problem. The NSS data indicate that 84.4 per cent of rural households are devoid of toilet facilities; in the case of urban areas it is 23 per cent.

The same scenario emerges if we look at the data on households with access to toilettes tabulated in the National Human Development Report, 2002, prepared by the planning Commission. In 1991, such facilities were enjoyed by only 9.48 per cent of rural household; in the case of urban households it was 63.85 per cent.

Policy-makers are of late talking about the introduction of technology to improve the quality of life of the people. Electricity is the basic requirement. In India, according to the data tabulated in HDR 2002, only 30.54 per cent of rural households had electricity; in the case of urban areas it was higher: 75.78 per cent.

The bias of the state in favour of urban areas is evident from the per capita expenditure on basic services. According to the estimate of the Eleventh Finance Commission, per capita expenditure on basic services in rural areas during 1977-98 was Rs. 24, but in urban areas it was Rs. 49. Rural India contributes 27 per cent to the GDP, but gets back only 5 per cent, which is less than one-fifth of its contribution.

Abusalef Shariff and others, in an article in Economic and Political Weekly (March 1, 2002), have shown that while the share of expenditure on urban poverty alleviation programmes in the total budgetary allocation by the Central government declined from 1 per cent to 0.8 per cent during the period between 1990-91 ad 2000-01, the per capita expenditure for urban poor increased from Rs. 11 to Rs. 28 during the same period. But for the rural poor, the per capita expenditure it is just one-eighth of this.

In a post-colonial capitalist country like India, uneven rural–urban development or rural–urban disparity is not unusual. While it is almost impossible to bring it to an end, it is possible to reduce the disparity to a tolerable level. It may be recalled that Gandhiji emphasized on rural growth and pleaded for village swaraj. He wanted the engine of India's development to start rolling down from the villages. But it became clear from the discussions in the Constituent Assembly that it would not happen. Dr. B.R. Ambedkar characterized village as "a sink of localism, ignorance and communalism". Nehru felt that villages were culturally backward and no progress could be made from such places. Urban bias was clearly reflected in the attitude of the policymakers. This seems to be continuing unabated.

In the Human Development Index prepared by the Planning Commission, there is a significant divide. The value for rural areas is 0.340, in the case of urban areas it is as high as 0.511. The index is a composite of variables capturing attainments in three dimensions of human development namely, economic, educational and health. The same is the situation in respect of the Human Poverty Index: rural 42.25 and urban 44.8.

Given the situation, what can be done to reduce the level of disparity to a desirable level is a matter that calls for serious consideration. There is no doubt that India's rural economy cannot grow without agricultural development. Capitalist agricultural productivity is constrained by the system itself. Effective land reform coupled with non-land input support to the beneficiaries can result in a increase in agricultural productivity.

Apart from taking steps to increase human development facilities in the villages, such as health and education, and develop appropriate infrastructure such as roads and marketing facilities, there is the need for generating employment, which can better the living conditions of villagers. We need to adopt a long-term policy, keeping in mind the requirements of the rural and urban areas. A close look at the development plan exercises tends to demonstrate that ad-hocism permeates the police processes.

In the rural areas there are many resources lying unutilized. It is time to identify these and make proper use of them. The application of Information Technology can be of great help in identifying what is lying unutilized or underutilized.

In West Bengal, it is being done in some rural and municipal areas. Jalpaiguri has done a remarkable job in this regard. It is the only district in the State to go in for participatory decentralized planning. Under this programme, the people themselves prepared village registers, electoral constituency-wise (gram sansad). These registers are mines of information, and they record the people's perceptions of development. The database is important for the development planning exercise.

Kerala has shown the way through the people's campaign for decentralized planning. Rural-urban disparity is the least in Kerala. There is a rural-urban continuum, rather than a divide. The people's campaign has definitely helped to make further improvement in the situation. The fact, however, remains that these steps at the State level, on matter how significant they are, cannot fully take care of the problem unless there is a shift of policy at the national level. This calls for sustained pressure from the bottom, that is, rural India. Secondly, urban development in a country like India has to dovetail with rural development. Otherwise, rural out-migration will upset the applecart.

Cultural Divide in Indian Cities

India's cities are hinges between its vast population spread across the countryside and the hectic tides of global economy, with its ruthlessly shifting tastes ad its ceaseless murmur of the pleasures and hazards of modernity. This three-cornered relationship decisively mould India's future economic, cultural and political possibilities. The demographic drift across the world is unstoppably towards the urban. "Modern India's political and economic experiences have coincided most dramatically in its cities—symbols of the uneven, hectic and contradictory character of the nation's modem life. From the ancient sacred space of Benares to the decaying colonial pomp of Calcutta, from the high rationalism of Chandigarh to the software utopia of Bangalore, from Bombay's uneasy blend of parochial politics and cosmopolitan to the thrusting new cities of the north. The evident urban dysjunctures have enlivened distinct political sentiments.

If is there a singular identity within a global context, when the world is shrinking and turning into a global village. The title itself is meant to provoke and tease both the practitioner and the viewer to relook at identify. It is singular? Multiple? dual? or even fused. Which intersections does it emphasized, which points of reference resonate? A globe called home, yet a search for imaginary homelands? A polyglot culture, where every being is in tumultuous transit between identities? Or composite identities, perhaps a current reality?

Art today becomes an exciting statement of the cultural diversity mapping diverse geographies. Homogeneity, which emerges as a by-product of globalization, leads to the growing importance of nudging the cultural producer to look for the celebration of the difference.

The trauma of post-modernism is that we seem to be everywhere at once; so many different position seem to be available to use in our perceptions of art. If we are living in the west, our journey may threaten to take us back in time and to transplant us to many locations on others parts of the globe. Art emerging from different areas have changed the trope of the debate, leading to a new emergence of ideas of internationalism, a new perspective a new difference in the reading and making of art history, a new exotica. Leading to issue concerning—plurality, heterogeneity, migration, travel, transculturation, contact zones, hybridity, de-territorialisation, re-territorialisation, identify, nationality and nationhood-that are at the forefront of artistic practice the world over. As a visual language, art melts barriers and, in the last few decades, there has been a definite move towards the macro-spaces of globality, bringing together artists on a plane where individuality celebrates differences.

In the case of diaspora, exiles, immigrants and emigrants, struggles with dislocation and recognition of the empowering potential remain a constant engagement. And within such a milieu, identity is not discovered but established by acts of self-representation that are political. Certain kinds of cultural forms had to be negotiated in the process of identity construction becoming, in the bargain, an establishment of differences as well as an accretion of experiences. Where the individual 'self' has become in itself a universal topic.

The post modern thought see 'identity' as something fragmentary and economic, rather than static. Seeing in this way the individual has different identities in different social situations. The questions of identity now orbit around the development of new identities and homogenous cultures which stand in contrast to the hybrid plural technical. Leading to tribulations of dislocation of identity and problems of identity fragmentation, the splintering of culture into diverse sub-cultures, the spread of mass-media culture, and the clash of social values. Identity is neither continuous nor continuously interrupted but constantly framed between the simultaneous vectors of similarity, continuity and difference.

This question of identity carries valence for artists particularly in the age of globalisation where boundaries are not so definite and the dynamic interactive process through diverse media takes precedence which is essentially observable in the virtual space that has shrunk the world to a small screen. Suggesting a brave new terrain where the poetry of visual arts often completed in the imagination of the viewer. Globalisation has been the tendency to treat history, culture and political economy as a world system with the possibility of reducing it to a single and unique point of view. Art today is becoming a living statement of the effect of globalizations and of the acceptance of the Diaspora by the host society. Signalling a shift away from the history of visual art as a single narrative which distinguishes itself from the inheritance of aesthetic traditions ad including in itself the demands of the twentieth century. Inhabiting itself in the 'now' of the increasingly common international biennales, with their gathering of diverse and maybe even incommensurable practices, generating communications and confusions in the mélange of practices from the disparate cultures; the 'now' of international exchanges today in business, politics, leisure and culture, operation though the power, speed ad relative availability of air travel and tele-technologies such as e-mail and web, the now in which different cultures and ethnicities face, meet or confront one another for all sorts of reasons, sometimes by choice and sometimes not, differentiating the boundaries and horizons of social and cultural bodies in the process, the now of economic globalization, the now of cultural, symbolic borrowings, appropriation, assimilation and transformation in the international context both at the individuals ad collective imaginaries. What it all proposes is a critical articulation of contemporary cultural practices and their presentation, and of what contemporaries might infect be. The immediate challenges are clear: bringing together artists from different geographical and cultural zones into a single exhibition space.

The new urban space is particularly well suited as a starting point for understanding contemporary India: The city is a crucially intricate construction born out of the intersection of diverse social, economic and cultural tempers, as a source of multi valiantly layered experiences, playing itself in various keys across diverse visual regimes, the city, now occupies the mind of the artists in various arresting poses.

The mega cities reflect the complex relation between globalization, local traditions and newly created spheres of life, and they allow contemporary art production, spiritual healing and body work, folk art and handicrafts, cinema and pop to coexist. Here we can see how traditional approaches are translated into contemporary forms of expression and how they are becoming established as widely influential in western circles.

In Indian cities today, the visual image—as seen on billboards, calendars, stickers, magazines, posters, in television broadcasts and films, in restaurants and shops, on the road side and on the façade of buildings on taxi's stocks and buses—plays a major role in the everyday of the people. It shapes their identities and moulds their personal and social values, thereby forging ideological conceptions of the nation itself.

Mumbai/Bombay, New Delhi, Bangalore and Calcutta/Kolkatta are not only among the mega-cities of the world they also represent increasingly important cultural intellectual centres. Here, a whole new world of images, sounds and gestures is evolving and gaining significance in India and abroad alike. Bollywood, Bhangra, beat and Asian dub are influencing global culture to an increasing extent, a lively contemporary art and theatre scene has developed in the past decades, and India has become home to a large number of outstanding intellectuals and authors of the art technology and ancient forms of culture which meet and merge in India.

Not only does this new emergence in art practices give India a new reading and making of art history, but it also creates a bridge between the cultural divide. A bringing in of a new trajectory, while retaining its cultural traditions. The Indian cultural sphere seems to be in a debate between conservative and the liberal, the revivalist and the progressive, the socialist and the consumerist, the indigenes and the international. Becoming for the artists' fraternity, a heightened difference make their creative experiences unique. The concept is replacing the image, and the process is diminishing the prominence of the product, where the questioning of the medium for its foreign origin is less important as more compelling questioning of the medium for its foreign origin is less important as more compelling questions become discussed. Art is 'now' portraying sensibilities and cultural specificities.

Against this backdrop of outburst and outpourings a new trajectory is emerging by ways of ideas, materials, processes and a breaking down of artistic genres. Where a new ideology is shaping and changing the landscape of contemporary art practices of today.

Art works cover a gamut in terms of their techniques and material as well in their forms of expression—from installations to digital prints to mixed media to watercolours to relief sculpture. Celebrating differences, the heterogeneity of concepts and their visualization by the artists makes dynamic references to borders crossed and recrossed. It (borders) marks a place that is the moment of difference becoming a source of productive excitement.

The artists in this exhibition are the voice of contemporary India-the visual culture which is encompassing the spirit of a nation which is finding its unique voice in the global, international world which has a cosmopolitan feel to it. A modernity, rural-urban, literacy-illiteracy, wealth-poverty.

The artists selected here for this exhibition suggest and use a post modern language, a multi-disciplinary approach, working in photography, installation and video. Their works work deal with issues of identity within a global context, particularly looking at the homogenizing effect of co modification in relation to developing economics. The projects undertaken by these eleven contemporary artists involve eclectic collecting, documenting and recycling of urban debris, looking at the mundane and the profane, The work critique the market forces that define the cultural and art practices of the peripheral nations and question how our identifies, within the global set up, can be sustained via a hybridization.

Bridging the Urban-Rural Divide

CAPART

The Council for Advancement of People's Action and Rural Technology (CAPART) was set up as a pioneer organization in September 1986, as a supporting and funding agency for the voluntary organization (Vos) by merging two organizations, namely, People's Action For Development (India) and Council For Advancement of Rural Technology (CART) with the mandate to promote voluntary action and propagate appropriate rural technologies for the benefit of the rural masses. Since then, CAPART has been contributing towards the rural development and poverty alleviation through the through the work of Vos at the grass roots level and by supplementing Government's efforts.

Organisational Set Up

The Minister for Rural Development, Government of India, is the President of the Council and Minister of State is the Chairman of the Executive Committee of the Council. The General Body comprises, not exceeding, 100 members representing voluntary agencies, Central and States Government and Institutions engaged in activities connected with Rural Development, Rural Technology and Individuals possessing experience/ expertise relevant to the furtherance of the aforesaid objectives of CAPART. They are nominated by the President of the Council. The Executive Committee of CAPART comprises a maximum of 25 members nominated by the President of CAPART from amongst the members of the General Body. There is also a Standing Committee on Finance and Appointments which is chaired by the Director General.

CAPART's finance, personnel and administrative matters, which require approval of the Executive Committee, are first considered by this Committee and then put up before the EC for approval.

The Director General (DG) is the Chief Executive of CAPART and is responsible for functioning of the Council. He is assisted in the discharge of these duties by two Deputy Director Generals (DDGs), Chief Vigilance Officer and Heads of Divisions at the Headquarters and Member Convenors (MCs) at the regional level. The total staff strength is 186.

Decentralization & Delegation

Prior to 1995, all the projects were sanctioned at the Head Office level thereby making it difficult to Monitor and Evaluate the progress. Therefore, for expediting the process of sanctions of projects and timely Monitoring and Evaluation, six Regional Offices were created at Ahemdabad, Bhubneshwar, Guwahati, Hyderabad, Jaipur and Lucknow and they started functioning from 1995 onwards.

Two Regional Offices were created at Chandigarh and Patna in 1998 and one Office at Dharwad in 1999. The Regional Committees (RCs) have been authorized to sanction project proposals upto an outlay of Rs. 20.00 laksh; monitor and evaluate all such projects within their respective regions; identify institutions for training of functionaries of voluntary organizations; maintain liaison and coordination with the concerned State Governments; and promote and develop small informal groups.

Emerging Project Profiles

In the initial stages, CAPART continued to implement the projects sanctioned by erstwhile PADI and CART.

Thereafter, CAPART undertook to implement various straight jacketed schemes like JRY, Housing, sanitation, Organization of Beneficiaries, Social Animator Training programme, DWCRA, ARWSP etc. till March 1999. During this period, funds were sanctioned under Central Rural Sanitation Programme, Drinking Water, Jawahar Rozgar Yojana and Housing Scheme and there was a mushrooming of Vos and growth of organizations which were not purely voluntary and participative. This resulted in a low level of people's participation and voluntary action. In order to give flexibility to these schemes and to discontinue schemes like IRDP, DWCRA which are being implemented by the State Governments, CAPART has switched over to the policy of financing three main schemes, namely, Promotion of Voluntary Action in Rural Development, Organisation of Beneficiaries (OB) and Advancement of Rural Technologies (ARTS). Apart from these three main schemes, CAPART also supports projects under Disability and Watershed Development. The Ministry has also provided budget to CAPART only under these three schemes since April, 1999. From 1.4.2001, budgetary support is being provided by the Ministry under one head namely "Assistance to CAPART" enabling CAPART to give emphasis on integrated and innovative projects, projects with people's participation, funding of good Vos and participation in disaster mitigation and rehabilitation work. It is stressed that the Policy Guidelines emphasizes a shift from funding Vos, if they are eligible, funding only 'good' Vos with the objective of setting up some 'models' of development rather than increasing expenditure for the sake of ensuring financial progress. This philosophy has brought about a qualitative change in funding the VOs.

Sanctioning Procedures

Voluntary Organizations which have been registered under Societies Registration Act, 1890, or State Amendment thereof, the Indian Trusts Act, 1882, or the Charitable and Religious Act, Companies Act, are eligible for support by CAPART. According to the Council's guidelines, such organization are also require to fulfill certain other prescribed criteria for funding. Any Voluntary Organisation falling within the eligibility criteria can directly apply to the council for support under different schemes by filling the prescribed forms. In the case of a first timer VO, it has to approach the concerned Regional Committee of CAPART with a project involving a modest outlay. If the proposal meets the norms and guidelines modest outlay. If the proposal meets the norms and guidelines of CAPART at desk appraisal stage, pre-funding evaluation is conducted during which the capability, credibility and community base of the organisation and the feasibility of the proposal are evaluated by an independent monitor. If the evaluation report is positive, the proposal is placed before the Regional Committee in the RCs/National Standing Committee (NSC) in the Headquarters for consideration. If proposal is not found to be according to the CAPART norms/guidelines or is not recommended by the project evaluators, even then, it is placed before the Regional Committee (RC)/ National Standing Committee (NSC) for rejection. Funds are released in installments depending upon the progress of the work and after evaluating the progress in the field by the evaluators. After the Project is completed, impact evaluation is also conducted to assess the impact of the programme and also ensure whether objectives of the projects have been achieved. Comprehensive impact assessment and post evaluation study by an independent professional body or team of experts/consultants is mandatory in all cases where a voluntary organization has been given assistance of more than Rs. 1 crore in a period of 4 years or Rs. 50 lakh for a single project. These reports are also placed before the concerned NSC and the Executive Committee.

Monitoring & Evaluation

CAPART has a system of monitoring and evaluation of the projects funded by it through empanelled project evaluators. As the quality of the project implemented depends upon close monitoring and timely mid-course corrective measures, the Council places great emphasis on monitoring and evaluation of the projects at different stages. Monitoring and Evaluation are generally done by external project evaluators on project to project basis from amongst the CAPART's panel of evaluators. CAPART's own officers, including Young Professionals, are also deputed to conduct these evaluations. Provisions are made to monitor projects at least at there stages i.e. pre-funding appraisal before release of funds in the second and subsequent phases and post-evaluation after the project has been completed.

A comprehensive panel of monitors has been drawn up for the purpose on the basis of their Curriculum Vitae, credentials and specialization. Experts from training intuitions as well as personnel from other organizations including the voluntary sector are requisitioned as Institutional monitors to evaluate some of the projects, where necessary.

Funding Restrictions

CAPART has evolved a comprehensive system for ensuring proper accountability of grants released by it to the voluntary organizations for implementation of development projects. In this regard, detailed policy guidelines have been laid down by the national Standing Committee on Monitoring and Evaluation which has been specifically constituted for the purpose.

Further Assistance Stopped

Whenever CAPART gets prima facie evidence that grants released by it have not been properly utilized by the VO or the promises implementation of the project, a temporary funding restriction, viz. Further Assistance Stopped (FAS) is imposed on the erring VO. The same can, however, be revoked by the concerned RC and the

Director General at CAPART, HQ if the VO removes all the deficiencies in project implantation.

Blacklisting

In case a VO is found to have indulged in financial misappropriation of CAPART grant, it can be placed in the Blacklist category as per the laid down guidelines and procedure. So far 273 VOs have been put in the blacklist category. Detailed guidelines have also been prepared for delisting of the VOs from the Blacklist category.

Transparency in the Functioning of CAPART

In order to introduce transparency in the functioning of CAPART, National Standing Committees (NSCs) have been set up at Head Office level and Regional Committees at the regional level which have been entrusted with the task of sanctioning projects. The Members of these Committees are drawn from the Voluntary Sector, specialized agencies of the Government, State Rural Development, who have fair idea of the voluntary organizations functioning in their respective areas. They are to ensure that funds are sanctioned to those organizations having a good track record of working with people's participation. The intimation of the sanction of the project is sent to the concerned District Collector and the Panchayat. CAPART's bimonthly newsletter also carries information pertaining to the details of projects sanctioned. Similarly, CAPART's home page (http//capart.nic.in) carries VO-wise details of the projects sanctioned to each of the VOs which is regularly updated.

Budget

The annual budget of CAPART during the last 3 years has been Rs.30 crore. Till 30th November 2002, as against the budget of Rs. 30 crore a sum of Rs. 30.96 crore has already been utilized. It is expected that in addition to the entire budget, the unspent balance of Rs. 13.60 crore available in the beginning of the year will also be utilized during the current years.

Activities

CAPART as a promoter of different models of Development has undertaken the following activities:

Rural Technology

Under Advancement of Rura. Technology, the broad mandate of CAPART is to coordinate all efforts towards advancement of technology relevant to rural areas except for sectors being dealt with by ICAR, CSIR and their sister organizations. The main objective of the Council under this Scheme is development, demonstration and dissemination of innovative rural technologies for the transfer to the target groups. Projects aimed at conducting need-based study, survey, skill up gradation, adaptive Research and Development, dissemination of appropriate technologies amongst rural poor and capacity building of the VOs are funded under this Scheme. A programme of setting up of Technology Resource Centres (TRCs0 was initiated by CAPART under this Scheme. Under this programme, voluntary agencies with proven track record of adaptive R&D and technologies transfer are supported with one time grant for creation of necessary infrastructure and some recurring expenses for development and dissemination of appropriate technologies through a network of small OVOs within their area of operation. CAPART has provided support to 19 VOs for Technology Resource Centres. Several TRC proposals are in pipeline. CAPART's objective is to set up at least on TRC in every state and eventually about 100 TRCs to cover all districts in India. CAPART has been participating in National Mission on Bamboo Development for promotion of cultivation of Bomboo outside the forest areas involving voluntary sector.

Public Cooperation Scheme

Under the Public Cooperation Scheme (PC), CAPART supports integrated rural development projects which are innovative and replicable. The thrust of the scheme is in involving the community in project design, planning, implementation and post project care and maintenance of the Assets created. These projects invariably focus on the disadvantaged rural strata with income ad employment generation as the basic concern.

Watershed Development Programme (WSD)

CAPART watershed programme is operational in drought prone and water scarce areas with the active involvement of grass root voluntary organizations and village level Beneficiaries. The Programme involves experienced voluntary organizations representing all the agro-ecological zones in the country. The capacity building stage in the Programme is very useful for the voluntary organization as well as for village level workers in the way that implementation adheres to the watershed principles, such as top to bottom and ridge to valley approach. When the Watershed Conservation and Development Programme was initiated by CAPART, it was felt that CAPART would be in a position to reach out to all the voluntary organization it was supporting. Therefore seven Support Voluntary Organizations (SVOs) were identified all over the country which had the required expertise ad recognition in the field or Watershed Development. It was decided that these SVOs would provided training to the VOs implementing CAPART watershed projects. It is also the responsibility of the SVOs to do the hand holding of such Project Implementing Agencies (PIAs) throughout the project cycle/ implementation phase. These SVOs act as extended arms of CAPART in the field.

At present 208 projects under Watershed Conservation and Development programme are being supported by CAPART all over the country.

On the basis of the project evaluators' (PEs) report, the NSC on Watershed approves the VO either in Track B or Track A. Those VOs with experience and expertise in water resource programmes are identified as Track A and inexperienced ones under Track B. The capacity building phase of about 6 months is provided to these VOs. All this is classed under pre-stage 1 after completion of which the Track B VOs graduate to Track A and are considered to be in stager I. Under both the category, the VOs undergo a mandatory Basic Training Course at the SVO during the first three months. Once the SVOs send the progress report of the concerned organizations, they are promoted to Track A. stage II is devoted towards compilation of action plan. Once done, such action plan is evaluated by a team of monitors and then subsequently placed before the NSC. The NSC then either sanctions or rejects the action plan. Thereafter, the project enters stage III which involves implementation of comprehensive action plan. All these activities are interspersed with the promotional workshops which are periodically held in different parts of the country. The involvement of SVOs and peoples participation is unique in CAPART's Watershed programme and this makes it different from other agencies funding ad supporting Watershed projects in the country. Various agencies such as NABARD have evinced a keen interest in the monitoring system evolved by the watershed division and want to emulate them.

Drought Proofing

Watershed division also looks after the Disaster

Management Projects, which are classified under Drought Proofing. Drought is a recurring phenomenon in large tracts of arid and semi arid zones of the country. This phenomenon is also observed in areas, which receive substantial rainfall. The probable causes for this are the inadequate and inappropriate water conservation measures. Hence the natural outcome of any instance of drought is the distress migration of the local community to distant areas in search of livelihood. In general, the objective of taking up such cases is to serve the short term goal through drought mitigation. Watershed division however stresses upon the long term sustainability aspect thought the projects. In the final analysis, it is the aim of the division to integrate the Drought Proofing projects with the core activity of Watershed Development.

Initiatives in Disaster Mitigation and Disaster Preparedness

CAPART has been playing a pro-active role wherever natural disaster has struck and adversely affected the rural population across the country. Some of the areas where CAPART has recently taken initiatives to provide assistance to the affected people through voluntary organisations, are the earth quake affected areas of Uttarakhand and super cyclone Rajasthan, Gujarat, Madhya Pradesh and Andhra Pradesh and the earthquake hit areas of Gujarat. CAPART has not only been providing relief assistance but has initiated long-term strategies to deal with this recurring natural phenomenon by people's action through the voluntary sector.

Organization of Beneficiaries

CAPART gives organization of beneficiaries of

antipoverty poverty Programmes due importance through this scheme. The objectives of this scheme are to create awareness among the rural poor, organize them into groups and strengthen their bargaining capabilities. Under this scheme CAPART has so far supported 3703 projects at a cost of Rs. 26.74 crores.

Disability Programme

The Disability Action Division was set up in 1995 in CAPART. CAPART views disability as a development issue rather than as a problem of health or welfare. The aim of this division is to change the development paradigm from one of charity to that of empowerment. It attempts to provide equal opportunity in rural development to people with disabilities and promote their full participation in all initiatives by supporting Community Based Rehabilitation (CBR) programmes for the differently disabled.

Marketing Development

CAPART introduced its Marketing Division in 1989 with a view to provide opportunities, exposure and sustainable Market linkages to rural producers covered under various income generation schemes of the Council.

The first step toward extending an overall Marketing Development was the organization of Gram Shree Melas, Gram Shree meaning 'The Wealth of Villages'. Gram Shree Mela is a gateway throught which rural producers come together to market their products, providing an opportunity to rural producers to sell their products directly in major markets, to interact with the buyers, to study and comprehend the latter's tastes, preferences and choices. Thus it helps them to upgrade and adjust their products and marketing skills and provide a better service to consumer while benefiting from a larger marketing opportunity. NSC approved a total of 14 Melas for the year 2002-03, out of which 5 Melas were held in 2002 at Hyderabad, Chennai, Ahmedabad, Mumbai and Bhubneswar respectively. The next schedule Melas upto March will be at Luck now, Ranchi, Chandigarh, Jaipur and Trivendrum. Apart from organizing/participating in regional/national level Melas, exhibitions, the Marketing Davison is also organizing a large exhibition under the banner 'SARAS' during the India International Trade held from 14th to 27th November every year. SARAS promotes the rural products manufactured by producers under the income generation schemes of the Ministry of Rural Development and CAPART ensuring a participation of over 15000 participants. SARAS 2002 bagged gold medal for the best display from India Trade Promotion Organization (ITPO) carrying forward the previous year's tradition . SARAS 2002 resulted in direct sales of more than Rs.4.50 crores ad the firm orders worth Rs. 2.00 crores.

In the year 2002, the Marketing Division participated in seven exhibitions at various places held from time to time. They are Panchayati Sammelan, Kisan Mela, SARAS, Rural Enterprise Sumit, Kartik Mela, Cattle Fair and Swadeshi exhibit in Kartik Mela (Ujjain) and Sonepur Fair (Bihar). Council is to participate in Magh Mela, North-East Trade and Industrial Fair in 2003.

International Funding

The International Funding Division receives funds mainly from one source i.e. UNDP. The GOI–UNDP sub-programme one energy was initiated in December 1999. The Ministry of Non–conventional Energy Sources in executive agency and CAPART is the channelising agency of the sub–programme. CAPART is implementing the sub–programme through the Society, Rural Industrialization,

Ranchi and Social Works and Research Centre, Tilonia. The Bihar energy sub–programme, "Energy Service for Rural Industrialization in Angara Block, Ranchi" aims to demonstrate Rural Industrial Area (RIA), provide energy services such as lighting, irrigation, agro-processing facilities etc. the total budget for the sub-programme is US$ 600,000 spread over three years. This programme has been extended upto June 2003 by the UNDP. The second energy sub-programme, title "demonstration of Community Based Solar Energy for Sustainable Development IND / 98/642 of UNDP", is being implemented by SWRC, Tilonia, Rajasthan. This sub-programme aims at demonstrating community based solar Photo-Voltaic (PV) systems in eight remote unelectrified village clusters in seven States of India—Rajasthan, Bihar, Himachal Pradesh, Madhya Pradesh, Sikkim, Jammu and Kashmir and Assam. The programme with a total budget of US$ 1.2 million is spread over three years. The sub programme activities have been extended upto September 2003 by the UNDP. Projects Sanctioned CAPART has sanctioned 386 projects involving a sum of Rs. 18.33 crore and released 26.76 crore during the year 2002-2003 (upto November 2002).

Media Division

ThMent Journalism etc.

Electronic Media

Under Electronic Media, the division has so far produced 57 films related to social issued. A database of information related to rural housing ad shelter was developed and is available on the Compact Disc (DC).

Management Information System Division

Management Information System Division (MISD) is

a support division. The division provides support to the project divisions in quick processing of information related to project files. The software package called Project Information and Monitoring Division (PIMS) has been designed under Oracle environment. This software is being maintained independently by Head Office and Regional offices. The databases provides information of partner voluntary organization, their projects ad details of evaluation of the sanctioned projects. The package has been decentralized and each user enters its own data. All the correspondence letters are generated through this system.

Apart from PIMS, Head Office is also maintaining an integrated database (CORP) which provides online information of VOs and Monitors. The micro level details are updated on weekly basis. This database has got a direct link to council's Website. The latest status of VO Monitors is available on Website.

5

Empowerment of Rural India

The idea that the Internet and related technologies might have an important role in aiding developmental efforts has captured a central place in international policy debates. Over the course of the last year, statements affirming the need to close the so-called 'digital divide' between social groups with several UN agencies, at the G-8 summit, and at meetings of developmental organization around the world. Many new websites now address this topic, and listserv hosts have moderated endless rounds of debated between digital enthusiasts and digital skeptics.

The idea of digitally oriented development is as powerful and seductive as the technology upon which it is based. No single technological revolution has changed the lives of current generation in the way that the internet has. No cultural-technological innovation since Television has had this kind of impact on the world's economy, its politics and its globalizing popular cultures, or even on our cultural conceptions of distance and time. The promise of digital development is that it might have the same reach as the original internet boom of the mid 1990s—only this time, the most disprivileged communities, those who had missed out on earlier waves of communities, those who had missed out on earlier waves of technology, might be able to 'leapfrog' over their more developed competitors.

The greatest obstacles to rural development—large distances and inadequate infrastructure—might be obviated by instant access to virtual institutions that provide banking, education, health care, neonatal information, agricultural advice, and so forth. But skeptics also have good reason. Bill Gates' now infamous dictum, that a computer cannot benefit someone earning less than a dollar a day, remains a serious challenge to any attempt to ameliorate social ad economic disparities through Information and Communications Technologies (ICTs).

In South Asia, where most rural populations lack running water and sanitation systems, where electricity is still a scarce and intermittent resource, where roads are poor and education a luxury these technologies truly appear to be far removed from the everyday concerns of the poorest sections of the countryside. This article critically examines the problems and possibilities of digital development in order to reveal the larger impact that ICTs could have on rural economies and societies.

Emergence of the Information and Communiications Sectors in India

As is well known by now, India's IT sector took off in the early 1980s with the establishment of off-shore development centers. Relatively cheap English-speaking engineering and technical talent were employed at centers in Bangalore and Chennai, then Heyderabad, and now in the suburbs of New Delhi (NOIDA). Since the liberalization of the Indian economy in the early 1990s, the Indian government has relentlessly promoted the IT sector as the harbinger of the nation's economic aspirations. Even though the country possesses only 3.7 million Personal Computer (PCs; Pentium I or superior), it houses the largest number of software professional outside California, whose efforts might result in the export of software worth 8 billion dollars next year, much of it to the United States.

As of 2001, the initial euphoria surrounding India's successful software export industry has given way to a new introspection into the reasons why these intellectual and human resources have not driven improvements in India's public and private institutions, education systems, and infrastructure.

These reasons are not hard to find: *(i)* the Indian software industry solves small components of large problems for international clients; *(ii)* this work is usually protected by confidentiality agreements; *(iii)* many India software professionals d companies compete for the same international contracts; *(iv)* the opportunity costs of working for Indian versus international clients is very high; and finally *(v)* low teledensity, computer usage, literacy the inadequacies or regional language software interfaces and other obstacles of India's developing infrastructure, coupled with regulatory hurdles have inhibited such ventures. None of this prevented Andhra Pradesh's Chief Minister Chandrababu Naidu from crafting an aggressive state policy to attract IT-c riented investments, simultaneously claiming that this sector served the larger public interest.

The constraints of electoral politics in India's largely rural society have meant that economically liberal and technologically sophisticated leaders could but afford to leave themselves open to the charge of promoting IT at the expense of rural development, and this is a fine line to walk: Even as he invited Microsoft to set up a software centre in the Hyderabad's technology park, Naidu also installed a highly sophisticated network of communications systems in his home constituency of Kuppam, as a model for other regions of the State. Beginning in 1996, he was the first Indian politician to advocate E-governance for making the state machinery more responsive and sensitive to citizen needs at the district and panchayat level.

As of 2000-01, these policies are being emulated at the national level through an 'IT for the Masses' policy statement, as well as a forthcoming policy statement on E-governance. Neighbouring Karnataka is one among may other states of India to have issued an IT policy statement directed towards the 'common man'. Naidu's solution to the political dilemma of promoting high-tech alongside rural empowerment, therefore, long anticipated current international debates on 'digital divide'.

Despite the on-going deregulation of India's telecommunications sector, its national teledensity (telephones per hundred persons) has improve very slowly, from .06 in 1990, to almost 3 today (compare with China at around 10). Voice over Internet Protocol (VoIP), and Wireless-in-Local-Loop (WiLL or WLL) technologies, however, now appear set to offer a cheaper and lighter form of telecom infrastructure, that should improve rural access exponentially.

New software and dictum start-ups have begun targeting non-English speaking users, and the idea of non-elites using and benefiting from ICTs has begun to gain currency. Nevertheless, the export-oriented software industry has yet to take full advantage of the opportunities presented by the Infotech and Telecom sectors in India could create a profound social and economic revolution in rural communities across South Asia.

The problems and potential of ICT-driven projects in South Asia are truly enormous. This region hosts an extraordinary concentration of new technology driven companies, tech-savvy administrators and manager, a political class newly sophisticated to the possibilities of IT, social entrepreneurs and NGO institutional structures that could all come together to bring the benefits of networked technologies to rural and disprivileged groups. And yet, we must face the frustrating of intermittent, inconsistent electrical power, archaic, scarce and unreliable telephony and net-connectivity, neo-feudal politico-business consortia that hinder or hijack developmental efforts, deeply ingrained ideologies of caste-hierarchy, gender inequality, and religious-communal difference, as well as significant derivations of basic human needs.

The limitation cast grave doubt over the optimism of those attempting to use emerging technologies for developmental purposes.

A common objection to IT initiatives suggests that they are premature, or that they 'put the cart before the horse,' in as much as electricity, telephony, and connectivity are highly erratic and variable in many parts of South Asia. Moreover, more basic kinds of infrastructure including schools, healthcare centers, balanced nutrition, gender equity, employment, and transportation are lacking. Why should we consider this expensive and elitist form of infrastructure, when more fundamental developmental needs remain unmet?

This criticism assumes that there is a standard sequence and hierarchy for development: first a society must adequately manage its nutrition and healthcare, then it must address education and achieve total literacy, then it must provide electricity to all its village, then it must install telephones, and so forth. In fact, post-colonial societies in Asia, Africa and the Americas have repeatedly shown that they can be successful in one or another dimension of human, social, and economic achievement, without necessarily replicating a normative European trajectory of industrial development.

Diverse social and infrastructure needs must be addressed more or less simultaneously to ensure a nation's future growth and prosperity. It is naïve to imagine that electricity, telephony and connectivity in rural areas will improve if the demand for these resources does not grow. In addition, information networks can become conduits that allow money to flow into the village through new kinds of non-discriminatory, clean and relatively unimpressive industries. Information and communications technologies can also compensate for other kinds of infrastructure limitations. For example, if online work, trade, or payment were to become available for members of a villager community, the poor quality of reads to and from that village becomes less of an obstacle to earnings and employment.

Finally, and most importantly, if capital were to become more readily available within a village community through such networked systems, it would then be in better position to finance the basic infrastructure that it needs, including roads, dispensaries, water and sanitation systems.

It may be correct to say that PCs remain expensive, fragile, quickly obsolete, English-centric, complex and difficult to master, and therefore almost entirely elite in their scope and operation. Nevertheless, networks of human-mediated community, could in fact prove to be the most inexpensive and inclusive form of rural infrastructure possible today.

Although this kind of a public information centre would require a hardware-cum-software-cum-connectivity investment of about Rs. 40,000 (appx. US$ 850), this resource could then serve between 500 and 5,000 citizen-consumers. The technology's cost per capita is therefore miniscule. The M.S. Swaminathan experiment in Pondicherry, and NIIT experiment in New Delhi's slums have demonstrated that even those with limited education, literacy, or English competency can quickly master windows-based point and click graphical user interfaces.

Moreover, the Gyandoot Project in Dhar, Madhya Pradesh, has demonstrated that rural citizen-consumers are quite willing to pay for the services of such centers, so long as these transactions make a direct and real impaction their life and livelihood. Here we may empirically disprove Bill Gates' theory that the most poor citizen-consumers will not encounter Microsoft or Wintel products: persons making less than $ 1 per day have regularly come into existing information centers to seek information on regional hospitals and medical centers, to send and receive emergency messages, and to transact with the state machinery in ways that enhance their quality of life and livelihood. Rural information networks can allow knowledge, services, money and certain kinds of products to more easily flow from node to node across long distances.

Each village node can also serve as a range of virtual institutions, such as a community centre, a bank, a medical centre, a government information centre, a matrimonial office, a public telephone booth, a public library ad educational resource centre, all at a fraction of the cost of corresponding 'real' institutions. By making these resources available in village, information centers can alleviate the asymmetry between urban and rural environments.

In order to accelerate rural growth, it is essential that we learn new ways of integrating social and human infrastructure development into the installation of basic information and communication infrastructure.

Overcoming Infrastructure Bottlenecks

The three basic infrastructure requirements for rural ICT initiatives are, of course: *(i)* Electricity, *(ii)* Telephony (or its equivalent), and *(iii)* Network Connectivity. The problems associated with these inputs must be recognized as inherent features of landscape, and tackled as an integral part of the implementation process.

(I) Electricity

In many rural areas, electrical supply may be restricted to only 6 or 8 hours a day. When electrical power is available, its voltage and frequency may vary far outside the acceptable limits of most hardware. Finally, there is often on earthing provide.

For most rural ICT projects, battery back-ups and Universal Power Supply-s (UPS-s) are mandatory. In some cases, multiple tractor batteries have been connected in parallel to create a mammoth UPS that can withstand day-long power cuts. In addition to these battery systems, circuit breakers ad voltage stabilizers are also necessary. Several agencies have had to create their own earthing pits outside their village centers, by digging shallow trenches, filling them with salt, and making sure they are watered on dry sunny days. Constant maintenance of this privately constructed earthing pit is necessary to ensure that the equipment within is protected from power surges.

(II) Telephony

Landline telephones are still not available in many villages in South Asia. Where they do exist they may be down for weeks at a time, and there may be other kinds of incompatibilities, which prevent data transfer. Several different kinds of short-term solutions are possible to circumvent low teledensity in rural areas.

A project in Pondicherry has implemented a wireless system for relatively slow data transfer using fax protocols. Short bursts of these wireless transmissions update the off-line content available at the village centre. The various educational enterprises of Zee Interactive Learning Systems plan to rely on Very Small Aperture Terminals (V-SATs), which connect directly to their own communications satellites. The Gyandoot project in Dhar, on the other hand, initially chose its target villages on the basis of their telephone accesses, and their location relative to proposed Optical-Fiber Cable (OFC).

Although it is possible to design rural ICT projects on the assumption that basic telephony will not be available, there is another, better, approach: Rural ICT projects may be used to infrastructure, including, for example Wireless-in-Local-Loop (WLL or WILL) technologies, which offer a cheaper, lighter, and more intelligent type of network. WLL systems allow simultaneous data and voice telephony across long distances (wireless), thanks to a local network of cables provided and maintained by a rural entrepreneur (local loop). Important applications of this technology have been developed at the TeNet Group at IIT-Madras.

(III) Connectivity

Internet subscription is not always available in rural and underdeveloped sections of South Asia. Even when it should, in theory, be available, long distance calls to nearby towns may be required in order to achieve true connectivity. Poor telephony ensures that modem speeds are often restricted to 28.8 kbps or slower. The wireless-fax system in Pondicherry runs even slower, at under 14.4 kbps.

While WLL technologies will soon be able to provide simultaneous and continuous voice and data connectivity in local areas, computer kiosks in villages can also be deigned so as to require only limited connectivity. Projects in Pondicherry and Warana, for example, allow users to access offline content, which is updated several times a day in brief bursts of data. In this way, a range of services may be continuously provided, notwithstanding narrow bandwidth, slow transfer rates, and intermittent connectivity.

Focus Areas for Development

In the following subsection we discuss the role of ICTs in different developmental sectors. Both urban and rural citizen consumers may benefit from ICT projects by receiving: *(i)* enhanced access to information and communication across large distance, *(ii)* improved access to governmental and quasi-governmental resources and services, *(iii)* opportunities to trade or bank online through kiosks, *(iv)* opportunities to design, manufacture and market their products through internet or intranet systems, *(v)* education through computers or about computers or both, and *(vi)* superior medical advice, diagnosis or knowledge in their own locality. This listing is by no means encyclopedic, and is intended only as a guide to the unfolding landscape. Social Investors and Social Entrepreneurs are invited to think of these resources as an incomplete tool-kit, or kit-of parts, that may be assembled together for new ad innovative applications, experiments, and project. Certain specialized application areas, including Global Information Systems (GIS), and Agri-input initiatives, for example, have been omitted for clarity and space.

Technology & Infrastructure Developments

The three major hurdles to the use of Information Technology in rural areas of South Asia have been: *(i)* inappropriate software *(ii)* expensive hardware and *(iii)* weak telecommunications infrastructure. In each of these fields, however, the landscape is slowly changing.

The Centre for the Development of Advanced Computing has been working on Indian language fonts and software for over a decade. Most state-sponsored IT initiatives, as well as many rural ICT projects, now use their fontographic standards, if not their text-processing software. In another significant development, a machine language translation project based in Hyderabad called Anusaraka promises to allow Indian language users translation between various Indian languages, as well as access to English language resources on the web.

As even occasional computer users will be aware, the cost of hardware is continuously falling, such that computers that were state-of-the art 3 or 4 years ago, are now available for a fraction of their original cost. Those computers—or, indeed, new computers configured just like them—are still good for basic text-processing, e-mail, and browsing functions. In addition, however, new entrants into the basic computing market such as the Simputer and the Station have been specifically designed for a mass market, including both urban and rural users. As mentioned above, Wireless-in-Local-Loop and related technologies have emerged as a cheaper, smarter form of telecom infrastructure, in comparison with traditional wire telephony.

The TeNet Group at the IIT-Madras has been at the frontline in developing technology solution designed to improve telecommunications infrastructure in rural areas. The group has incubated several companies that work up and down the value chain in this sector, including, most recently, n-Logue Communications, which is working as a rural internet service provider.

Rural Connectivity

Several projects now attempting to provide information and services to rural citizen-consumers via human mediated intranet systems. The Village Knowledge Centres Project run by M.S. Swaminathan Research Foundation in Pondicherry represents an early experiment in providing information and knowledge resources to rural communities.

The project uses wireless radios (CB radio; not to be confused with WLL) for data and analog voice transmissions between a semi-urban hub centre and eight village centers. At each village centre, offline content is updated through routine transmission using fax protocols. Although the project displays outstanding sensitivity to context, as well as gender and social equity, and has conducted pioneering participatory experimentation and documentation, it has not developed a strong economic model to ensure the financial sustainability of the project. For this reason, it is also inhibited from scaling up its experiment to include a larger section of the countryside.

The Warana Wired Village project is based in and around Warananagar, on either side of the Warana river in Maharashtra. Since the 1940s, these Cooperatives have been engaged in sugar refining, dairy processing, banking ad retail. The Prime Minister's Office (PMO) through the

National Informatics Centre (NIC) and the Government of Maharashtra collaborated with these Cooperatives, to fund an astonishingly dense and expensive network of fibre-optic cables, V-STAs, PCs, modems and servers which is estimated to have cost over 5 crores.

Although a number of different products and services were promised, this enormous infrastructural investment currently serves only as a distributed accounts system for the Warana sugarcane cooperative. Member of the cooperative may check that the tractor-loads of sugarcane they sent in were correctly credited to their accounts. Many lessons remain to be learnt from the limited returns from this project-principally the need for social research followed by a clear-headed cost–benefit evaluation of investments made into a rural ICT project.

The Gyandoot Project in Dhar, M.P., on the other hand, has emerged as a benchmark for innovation in the e-commerce and egovernance service it provides, as well as its business model. The project was initiated by members of the Indian Administrative Services (IAS) in consultation with various gram panchayats, which were selected as locations for village booths. Village panchayats paid for the equipment and space for kiosks called *soochanalayas,* which are operated by *soochaks,* who were selected and trained from among the unemployed educated youth of the village.

The Gyandoot team has also worked hard on providing the back-office support that is required to make these services relevant and useful for rural citizen-consumers. Further scalability will rely on the installation of WLL based internet League Communications incubated out of TeNet group at IIT-Madras is now providing connectivity for a series of new projects across India, including those in Madurai and Nellikuppam, TN, and Sikar, Rajasthan. The company works on a commercial basis in partnership with various local partners, including entrepreneurs and non-governmental organizations.

TARAhaat.Com., promoted by Delhi-based Development Alternatives, is an extremely ambitious commercial project to provide online services to a large number of rural communities in north India. One of the more innovative aspects of this project is its highly interactive and graphics-intensive interface system, which allows semi-literate and neo-literate users enhanced access to products and services. The organization had initiated information centers in several locations in Bundelkhand, M.P., and Bhatinda, Punjab, of which the later are still functioning. While the project will provide a menu of services that is similar, in many ways, to other rural ICT projects its current business model requires an astonishing influx of capital before it becomes self-sufficient.

The NIIT 'Hole-in-thee-wall' initiatives consists of unattended point-and-click devices in urban slums. In early 1999, Sugata Mitra set up an unmanned computer with a track ball in a slum adjoining the New Delhi offices of NIIT Limited, the major software development and research company. Continuous vide tape monitoring of the computer showed that young boys and girls from the settlement became highly proficient at suing the graphic interface, and in surfing parts of the web, notwithstanding limitations of language and training. The social and economic returns of setting up such unattended systems are yet to be fully comprehended. While these initiatives represent diverse approaches to the question of wiring rural India, several trends can now be observed: First, economically responsible projects are already proving more successful than charitable or free models. Second, projects that identify and cost the services they provide are also more successful. Third, an intimate understanding of the social and economic parameters of rural India gives connectivity provides a significant advantage. Fourth, WLL systems appear to be emerging as the infrastructure solution of choice.

E-Governance

The Gyandoot Project in Dhar, M.P., has developed a very important e-governance protocol, in the form of the shikayat, or complaint. For a fee of Rs. 10, rural citizens may select from a predetermined menu of 30 different kinds of complaints, which together over a wide range of citizen-consumer to government interactions in rural areas. These include for example: the absence of a school teacher; the death of a head of cattle that may require a government veterinarian; the malfunction of a public hand-pump that must be repaired, and so forth. Although this project has established only about 30 village centers so far, the number of complaints and requests that come pouring in every day has put enormous pressure on the office of the zila panchayat to redesign and to wire up its own back office systems, so as to keep pace with this demand. The lesson here is that E-Governance will be pulled into existence and operation through citizen-consumer demand.

The Andhra Pradesh government is responsible for some early initiatives that sought to use networked technologies to improve citizen services. A series of catchily-acronymed services including CARD, TWINS, FAST, etc. provide licenses and certificates, allow the registration of deeds, and various kinds of payments at a single counter, in certain urban and rural areas of the state.

'Bhoomi' is major Government of Karnataka initiative to computerize land records across the state. About a quarter of the state's taluka-s, or sub-districts, have now been computerized. At specified government offices in these districts, citizen-consumers may receive printouts of their land holdings with a schematic plan of their property on the obverse face. The computerization of these land records is an expensive, laborious and time-intensive process, as the online system must: *(i)* aggregate several different types of traditional village record-keeping, and *(ii)* provide a real time record of landholdings, so that they may have unimpeachable legal standing.

Wired Microcredit/ Microfinance/ Microcommerce

There is no doubt that the computerization of microfinance and microcredit records could result in savings of time and effort, and generally facilitate the maintenance of these accounts. However, the real transformative effect of this technology will be seen only once microcredit accounts come to be used for online or distance transactions amongst or within village communities at the grass-roots. This will allow rural entrepreneurs and craftspersons the same savings of time, travel, ad effort, that the Internet has afforded individuals and institution in the industrialized world. These possibilities have not yet been charted in any rural ICT project. The Swayma Krishi Sangam (SKS) project is recording transactional information on optical ID cards for microfinance, as well as for education and healthcare. Dr. Mohammed Yunus, Founder of the Grameen Bank of Bangladesh has notably called for the establishment of an 'International Centre for Information Technology for the Elimination of Global Poverty'. A related agency, Grameen Telecom has attempted to provide mobile telephones to rural consumers through existing MFI / MIC networks.

IT-Enabled Artisanal Industries

In addition to facilitating the flow of capital across rural areas, online financial and commercial systems could also provide the capital and infrastructure for new kinds of IT-enabled industries, in fields such as regional language data entry, Computer-Aided Design (CAD), and Computer-Aided Manufacture (CAM). These applications of information technology, of course, will only become possible on a large-scale once rural ICT projects are better established in the landscape. The Asian Centre for Entrepreneurial Initiatives has made an early attempt to introduce CAD/ CAM technologies to artisans in north Karnataka, alongside online advertising and sales.

Computer Training and IT-Enabled Education

So, for computer–training and IT-enabled education has been distressingly conflated ad confused in the understanding of administrators and policy makers as well as the general public. Most commercial providers, moreover, are involved in both sectors, and aggressively cross-market themselves.

Pratham Akshara and The e-Learning Centre together represent the most important attempt to create IT-enabled learning software for disprivileged children. They have developed educational games, which are now being tested in several rural areas through the Centre for Knowledge Societies, Bangalore. In Karnataka, 1000 rural schools are to be computerized private operators, including NIIT.

School Net India, the educational infrastructure wing of Infrastructure Leasing and Financial Services (IL & FS), is building multilingual educational content online, as well as CD-ROMs for use by teachers as a supplement to classroom education. Gurucool and Zee Interactive Learning Systems represent commercial attempts to provide online educational resources coupled with products ranging from in-class instruction to interactive CD-ROMs, to cable–TV programme. These products are predominately in English, although regional language translations could become widely available in future.

Tele-Health

Computer-based and Online expert diagnostic systems could enhance the quality of healthcare and diagnosis available to rural citizen-consumers in many remote parts of South Asia. The real benefits of these systems, however, may be the collation of more comprehensive public health information. In addition to tracking the case study of an individual patient, therefore, such systems could also collect data on the public health in a region, for further epidemiological study. The George Foundation has experimented with an expert diagnostic programme on a free standing PC in Dharmapuri district of Tamil Nadu. Other initiatives by privately run hospitals are in the planning stages.

Research, Advocacy and Consultancy Resources

Non-profit industry groups such as India's National Association of Software and Service Companies have served as advocates against policy regulations that might inhibit the growth of bandwidth and connectivity in South Asia. Their website hosts important statistics and information in the on India's internet economy, as does Inomy. Com. Bytes For All.Org is a voluntary online community that shares information with other web-oriented a advocates across South Asia. The NGO Voices serves as a research and capacity-building resource for community radio, and is beginning to experiment with the interface between internet and radio. Mahiti.Org a branch of the NGO Samuhua provides IT-services for NGOs in Bangalore area. The Centre for Knowledge Societies, Bangalore has collected socio-economic data on many of the projects mentioned above, and is also providing research and consultancy service for some of the developmental organizations.

Potential Impact on Rural Economics and Societies

Up until this point ICTs have been largely understood as a new kind of media or telecommunications infrastructure, which allows the dissemination of information, commands, or even education across distances. Developmental ICT projects, therefore, have attempted to assist rural communities by providing them news, information, advice, and knowledge which has hitherto been inaccessible to them. These kinds of inputs have allowed rural citizen-consumers to make more informed economic decision: farmers can decide whether to sell there produce locally or transport it themselves further a field; landless labourers have been able to negotiate their daily wage more effectively; tractors, threshers, old television sets, cattle and motorcycles have all been traded across towns and villages thanks to online advertisements.

However, rural ICT projects are yet to effectively position themselves as a vehicle for online commerce and a mechanism of employment for village communities. The first step in this direction would be to put rural Self-Help Groups (SHGs) and other Micro-Credit/Micro-Finance Initiatives (MCIs/MKFLs) online. This abstraction of cash money onto a online financial system would lay the groundwork for a new kind to rural e-commerce, which could prove extremely enabling for many communities, especially non-agricultural artisanal groups. Entrepreneurs and small-scale industries might then be able to regularize exiting off-line trade relationship into online systems that track raw materials, designs, quality control, and delivery mechanisms. New kinds of banking and finance systems in rural areas would make capital more easily available for investment into new businesses and rural infrastructure.

While persons making less than a dollar a day might immediately benefit only by having access to a more efficient and easily accessible form of banking, in the long run unemployed and underemployed poor would experience the significant secondary benefits of actually having access to a far better develop economy and the range of education, employment, and self-empowerment opportunities available therein. These possibilities can only be actualized once significant sections of rural South Asia achieve connectivity with one another and with the world at large.

Despite the economic promise of ICTs, their social benefits may not emerge immediately. According to a preliminary estimate prepared by the Centre for Knowledge Societies, Bangalore, the immediate impact of ICT projects upon their rural contexts will be far from equitable. Rather, ICT access is likely to increase socioeconomic opportunities for dominant caste landholding elites, relatively disprivileging non-elite non-landholding artisanal communities. There are several reasons for this:

Access to Capital Resources

Landholding groups always have access to capital in the form of land, which they can sell to start a business, move to the city, rent, etc. Even if they keep the land, their agricultural incomes will always be higher than the non-agricultural incomes of landless groups.

(i) Literacy and Education

Dominant caste agricultural communities tend to have higher literacy and education levels relative to disprivileged artisanal groups. Moreover, there are many young men and women, who may have completed secondary school, or failed out of college. Member of this class are likely to be the first beneficiaries of ICT-driven rural education, training, and employment opportunities.

(ii) Agricultural Technologies

States like Karnataka and Andhra Pradesh are racing to develop Agri-biotech and infotech policies and projects, in order to demonstrate that emerging technologies can actually help rural communities. All of these technologies will only serve to further advantage rural elites who have significant landholdings and enjoy a agricultural surplus.

The net effect of all these factors will be that most of the new entrants into South Asia's middle classes will come from rural landowning communities. Artisanal groups, Dalits, Adivasis and other disprivileged group will be relatively disabled from taking advantage of the opportunities offered by rural connectivity. In fact, there groups may be further discriminated against: *(i)* directly, through harassment or impeded access to networked facilities, *(ii)* indirectly, on account of the cultural, institutional or otherwise embedded prejudices of the hardware, software, or services offered.

On solution is to guide market forces such that they work against direct social or communal is crimination due to neofeudal village socioeconomic relations. This possibility might be best illustrated through a counter-example: A village computer is set up in a dominant caste household. The project is designed in such a manner as to expect zero financial returns on this equipment. The family is never taught to charge visitors for telephone or computer access. They therefore begin to think of the machine as their private entitlement, ad prevent Dalits from entering the centre or using its facilities. In a fracas prompted by this discrimination, some of the machinery is damaged and the centre is closed down. Similar examples are to be found all across the subcontinent, from Punjab to Tamil Nadu. What do we learn from this case? *(i)* Setting up public access devices in private homes is a poor idea. Like temples, shrines and sacral spaces, private residences are highly graduated spaces where some socials differences are immediately marked. It is far preferable that rural information centers be located in retail or market environments, where social differences are less accentuated. *(ii)* Charging for access and for various online transactions and services creates value for both provider and user. It allows them to enter into an economic relation such that the provider seeks to maximize computer access, allowing he profit motive to supercede hierarchy or communal difference.

Indirect social discrimination is more difficult to address, as the elite ad urbanc personalities who often design rural ICT Projects are likely to encounter and work with rural elites when they visit the field. This can result in a skewing of priorities in favour or rural elites and semi-elites and against artisanal and adivasi communities in the same area. In one project, members of adivasi communities rarely visited information centers, even though they comprised upto 40% of the project population. This was not only due to their relative economic impoverishment, but also because the available services were more precisely calibrated with the cultural assumptions and economic needs of local Dominant Caste and Bahujan communities.

No immediate solution presents itself for asymmetries caused by economic disprivilege. Nevertheless, it is possible first of all to ensure that these are not compounded by socio cultural discrimination, and secondly to plan for the expanded use of rural networked resources by lowering costs as soon as economies of scale and network effects emerge from an increasing subscriber base.

It is of the utmost importance that rural ICT projects be carefully designed with a view to enabling and including the very rural non-elite non-agricultural communities which are most likely to be left out. Information Design, which encompasses everything from the pattern of the sweater worn by the kiosk operator, to the architectural space of the information centre, to the hardware and software design, to the content, language, accent and fontography of audiovisual interfaces, to the very services which are available at the centre, together make the critical difference between exclusivist, empowering projects and exclusivist, elitist information centers. Funding organization and policy makers can encourage innovations in Information Design by stipulating that their projects routinely undergo socioeconomic impact analyses by specialist external agencies that have demonstrated their understanding of rural socioeconomic relations, and the potential impact that ICTs may have upon them.

For Future Digital Development

As indicated in the sections preceding, non-elite, rural, artisanal and adivasi communities of South Asia do not and will into use information and communication in exactly the same ways as industrialized nations elsewhere in the world. In order to find ways for emerging technologies to truly benefit these groups we must invent and innovate from the ground up, working always in partnership and dialogue with local communities. Far from replicating the online behaviour of highly connected and cosmopolitan societies in North America, Europe, or South East Asia, therefore, digital development in India requires us to design products, services, and technologies that solve very local problems and ameliorated local socioeconomic conditions.

Digital development affords a new perspective from which to imagine the future direction of India's political economy. Rather than remaining locked in the paradigm of an eternally developing nation, it now seems possible to aspire to becoming a knowledge society. Should India become successful in achieving such an empirical ad epistemic shift, this could eventually serve as a model for other emerging economies around the world. Before this can begin to happen, however, mutual realignments among the major estates of society—the state, private enterprise, academia, civil society organizations and global state agencies. Moreover, public discourse and policy debate must proceed from a new perspective, which recognizes emerging technologies as a profoundly important resource for public practice.

This vision can be achieved in may ways, but most easily through the direct perception of the world changing around us. I recently surveyed a semi-arid district in Rajasthan, and was surprised to discover a spate of new computer training centers: NIIT, Aptech, SSI, Compucom, MAHE, MICE.... The franchised outlets seemed to go on and on. We finally guestimated that there were about 100 computer–training institutes in this sparsely populated district, which might fall in the bottom quarter of human and social development ranking across India. All of these training centres were self-financing, and indeed, had been set up with a express profit motive. These centers reported high enrollments and placements, despite the near total absence of reliable connectivity all across the district. We also enumerated other existing institutions that could be computerized, or where information kiosks could be located: we counted 1500 sites including medical stores, village cooperatives, gram panchayat offices, mandi yards, and secondary schools, among others. There should be no doubt in any policy-maker's mind that there is a strong demand for network connectivity in rural India, and that the institutional infrastructure to make use of it already exists.

Some of the arguments against information–oriented development reflect the fears and anxieties of our own elite, not all of which is computer literate, of which only a few really understand the socioeconomic ramifications of information technology. Many recoil against the idea of digital development not only because the technology remains alien and intimidating to them, but also because they cannot abide the thought of their social inferiors achieving a literacy that they have not. While there are only a few who would openly oppose empowering information resources because of the threat to their social privilege, such hierarchical ideologies sometimes lurk under the surface of apparently utilitarian objections to information-oriented development.

The ideologies are refracted in different ways through agents in different estates of society. Representatives of activist NGOs and people's movements initiated in the 1970s for example, appear excessively suspicious of the role of private capital in driving technological development. They have not always had the opportunity pursue online cooperative models, such as internet advocacy and discussion groups, freeware, Linux and open source technology, or any of the other challenges to technological monopolies that have emerged through the network revolution. Unfortunately, it is the social expertise of the NGO sector-including their knowledge of village economics, social hierarchy and gender asymmetries—

that is most needed to ensure that rural ICTs function in ways that are maximally empowering and socially equitable.

At every public conference, trade show and media opportunity, scions of major Indian corporate houses dilate on the empowering effects of IT and its role in alleviating poverty. These homilies are rarely, if ever, backed up either by profit-driven infrastructure projects in rural areas, or by indirect philanthropic contributions. India's social sector and grassroots activists will therefore be forgiven for doubting the commitment of the IT sector, ad large corporates in general, to actually achieving rural development and economic empowerment. Nevertheless, by working in collaboration with academia and the NGO sector, I believe that venture capital can be invested for the creation of social infrastructure that can drive further growth. In this way, the corporate sector can serve the public good while also developing large markets for hardware, software, and connectivity in rural India. It is more and more plausible that social investment projects—which seek financial as well as social returns on their investment—are the swiftest way to create economic prosperity and social empowerment across rural India.

When I began estimating the potential impact of ICT projects in rural South Asia, I'd guessed that the three large southern states, Karnataka, Andhra and Tamil Nadu, would take the lead in bringing networked technologies to rural areas. At it has turned out, only Tamil Nadu hosts any rural ICT projects, and there too it is the non-governmental and private sectors that have initiated and driven these projects. By contrast, the state governments of Maharashtra and Madhya Pradesh have undertaken such initiatives, while Rajasthan, Chattisgarh, and Uttaranchal governments have similar plans afoot. On preliminary evidence, therefore, it appears that states with the most developed IT sector are lagging behind governments with no local IT sector are lagging behind governments with no local IT industry. Another indication of this divide is to be read out from between the lines of different state governments' IT policy statements: while the three southern states (alongside Delhi and Haryana) are better prepared to attract multinational investment, some of the progressive states in the Hindi belt have produced excellent policy documents that very effectively outline the government's plans for rural connectivity, e-governance, education, and all round e-development. It is not all that difficult to explain this conundrum: the work profile of the IT-Secretariat, in an IT-rich state is very different from its counterpart in an IT-poor state.

The former must attract investment, sell the state at road-shows in the US and Europe, liaise with CII. TIE, NASSCOM and other industry groups, plan and host trade shows, and even promote Biotech as the next wave. The latter, on the other hand, has only one mandate for the moment: computerize the state machinery and leverage IT to the political advantage of the incumbent government. Civil servants at every level, in my experience, are actually more curious and engaged with the possibilities of e-governance than is commonly believed. As with any other social sample, of course, particular members of the bureaucracy display fare greater ability to respond and adapt to changing technology than others.

Any developmental ICT project that involves the state apparatus will therefore be subject to not only to the variable aptitudes of the officers concerned, but also to the vicissitudes of cadre politics that rattles officers around into wildly disparate job descriptions without warning. The profile and prerequisites of the managing director of a state IT Public Sector Undertaking (PSU) for example, has little in common with that of a district collector. In the mid-eighties, Rajiv Gandhi's flawed solution to the problem of computer illiteracy in the bureaucracy was to post District and State Information Officers (SIOs) in every state, all reporting directly to the centrally controlled

National Informatics Centre. This had the effect of creating a new caste of officers who are effectively outside the control of the state administration, who sometimes seek to monopolize information access within their office, rather than disseminating it more widely into the administrative machinery of their district. More often than not, the DIO is still the only government officer at the district level with an official email address.

The various state Infotech PSUS that IAS officers lead also lack any certain mandate; they are expected to firefight every problem pertaining to IT, from rewiring the computers in the Chief Minister's house, to reviewing technology purchases for every department of the bureaucracy, to negotiating networking infrastructure with corporate entities. They are given by hierarchical striations, union cliques ad political interference, all of which inhibits the minimal creativity and initiative that is necessary to keep pace with current rates of technological obsolescence. These PSUs urgently need to be reorganized as financially responsible corporate entities run by non-cadre executive officers with a clear mandate to build information and communications infrastructure for India's people and their governments.

Although administrators and bureaucrats remain generalists, almost by definition, whether in South Asia or in any other part of the world, the difference here lies in the assumption of executive infallibility, and the lack of institutional relations with scholars, intellectuals, and knowledge workers. The state machinery must learn to rely on the knowledge and expertise of academy and NGO sectors, and employ the some of the new resources listed above, as well as those of the newly inaugurated Media Labs Asia. They must seek professional expertise in using new mapping, planning and data management technologies, such as Global Information Systems and Global Positioning System (GIS/GPS), for the design and documentation or rural development policy and programmes.

To effectively diver digital development in India, therefore, we need a new pattern of interaction between the different estates of our society, so as to maximally utilize their respective expertise and abilities. We will need: *(i)* well funded centers for research into technology, media of development, governance, and business can be generated, *(ii)* venture capital funds and new hybrid public-private corporate entities directed towards the development of social and human infrastructure, *(iii)* authoritative and responsible civil society organization that work with, rather than either against or in parallel with the state and private sectors, and *(iv)* governments and bureaucracies that work in transparent dialogue with these other states.

6

Government Policies on Micro and Small Medium Enterprises in India

Introduction

In India, there exists no definition of medium enterprises and as such, there is no specific definition for small and medium enterprise (SMEs). What prevails here is only the concept of small scale, ancillary and tiny industry which are related to related to the historical value of the investment in plant and machinery.

In other countries, SMEs are defined on the basis of both quantitative and qualitative elements, such as, the number of workers employed and/or annual turnover or the level of fixed investment. However, employment is an omnipresent criterion for determining the size of the unit in these countries. The prevailing definitions in some countries are listed in Table 6.1.

Importance of MSES

The khadi, village and small-scale industries have a

very important role in the Indian economy characterized by its vast spatial spread, unemployment and underemployment, rapidly rising labour force, capital scarcity, numerous market segments and diverse demand patterns, broad and diverse resource has and supply, predominance of widely scattered numerous village settlements, growing modern large industrial sector giving scope for an cillarisation and so on.

The distinguishing features ad major advantages of these industries particularly khadi and village industries, are the following:

1. In an economy, like India, characterized by abundant labour supply and the concomitant unemployment and underemployment and rapidly rising labour fore, khadi, village and small industries assume special significance because of its high employment potential.
2. Another major advantage is their ability to provide employment in the off-season. To a large number of people, agriculture provides only seasonal employment. Khadi, cottage and some other village industries provide employment opportunities during the off-season and help may households to mitigate their problems during the off-season.
3. Khadi, cottage and certain other village industries provide vast scope for employment of special categories of people like women, children, old aged, physically handicapped, etc. It is also an avenue for part-time employment for those who are employed elsewhere, either full-time or part-time.
4. Some of these industries provide employment opportunities within the household premises and some others near the place of residence. The vocational advantage of these industries are, thus, very great.
5. A major advantage of these industries is that the capital-output and capital-labour ratios are

comparatively very low. That is, the amount of capital investment required per unit of employment and the capital investment required per unit of output are comparatively very low. In other words, the khadi and village industries in particular and the small-scale unites in general maximize employment and output for a given amount of capital. This is of particular importance to a labour-abundant and capital-scarce economics.

6. Because of the low capital-output ratio and low gestation period they promote non-inflationary growth.
7. Khadi and village industries have been found to be of particular help to the weaker sections of the society. The participation of the scheduled castes, scheduled tribes, women and other weaker sections of the society in this sector is significant.
8. These industries promote economizing of resource utilization and conservation of resources. They are expected to ensure maximum utilization of locally available raw materials are used, thereby converting waste into wealth.
9. These industries can develop in almost all areas including backward, tribal, hilly and inaccessible areas. They are, thus, helpful in achieving wider spatial dispersal of industrial activities ad thereby reducing the regional economic imbalances.
10. They help increase the pace of rural development through the generation of additional employment opportunities and income and through its inputs and output linkages with the other sectors of the rural economy.
11. The small industries have acquired more attention in recent years due to the very less ecological problems they create, compared to the large industries.

12. As khadi and village industries do not use or use only very little electric power or oil, they do not cause energy crisis and foreign exchange crisis.
13. The fact that the village and small industries account for about one-third of our total export earning shows how important they are to the Indian economy constrained by shortage of foreign exchange.

Promotional Measures

A number of measures have been taken by the governments, central and state, to protect this sector from the onslaught of the large sector and to promote its growth.

Measures taken by the Government, from time to time, include reservations, upward revision of investment ceilings in the definition, reservation of products for the SSIs, increasing credit flows, preference in Government purchases, modernization, technology gradation and improving export performance.

In the post-reform period, a number of new steps have been initiated by the Government with regard to foreign direct investment, development of infrastructural facilities, establishment of growth centers, export promotion, marketing, etc.

The important protective and promotional measures include the following:

1. *Reservation of products:* Protection has been provided to the small-scale units by the reservation of items of exclusive production in the small scale sector. Over the years there had been an increase in the number of items so reserve, but has significantly reduced it recently.
2. *Reservation and Preference in Government Procurement:* SSIs have been given protection from competition in the matter of purchases of different products by the DGS & D. A large number of items have

been reserved for exclusive purchase from the VSI sector while a number of items have been provided price preference up to 15 per cent over units in the large scale sector.

3. *Infrastructural and Institutional Support:* Infrastructural and institutional supports are provided through industrial estates, district industries centers (DICs), Small Industries Service Institute, Khadi and Village Industries Commission (KVIC) and other specialized institutions which provide technical assistance, testing facilities, etc.
4. *Machinery on Hire Purchase:* The National Small Industries Corporation (CNSIC) arranges supply of machines on hire purchase to small scale units.
5. *Marketing Assistance:* Marketing assistances including export promotion assistance are provided by institutions such as the NSIC, the Small Industries Development Organization (SIDO), Handicrafts and Handlooms Export Promotion Corporation, KVIC etc.
6. *Financial Assistance:* Financial assistance is provided at concessional terms by commercial banks, state level financial institutions, etc. In order to step up the flow of assistance to the small sector ad to provide a focal point to coordinate at the apex level the availability of both financial and non-financial inputs required for the orderly growth of this sector, the Small Industries Development Bank of India (SIDBI) was established in 1990.
7. *Training:* Training for existing and potential entrepreneurs and other associated with the working of the small units are offered by entrepreneurship Development Institute of India (EDII), Technical Consultancy Organisation (TCOs), financial institution and commercial banks, management institute, NSIC etc.

8. *Supply of Raw Materials:* Arrangements have also been made for the supply of raw materials, particularly of scarce items, to the small scale units.
9. *Promotion of Ancillarisation:* The Industrial policy also gives importance to ancillarisation. This has been recognized as one of the objective of the public sector industry. One of the factors considered by the government while evaluating applicant ion from the private sector for industrial licence was the scope for ancillarisation by proposed project.

A more detailed account of some of the promotional aspects is given below.

Industrial Estates (IE) Programme

With a view to encouraging entrepreneurs to set up small industries and to expand existing unity, a programme for the establishment of industrial estates was starter in the year 1955. This programme envisaged the following facilities for entrepreneurs: *(i)* the acquisition of suitable land and its development; *(ii)* the construction of factory sheds; *(iii)* the provision infrastructure like water, electricity, transport, banks, canteens, watch and ward, all-weather approach roads.

The important objectives of this programme were to: *(i)* facilitate the growth of SSIs; *(ii)* shift industries from congested areas to estate premises; *(iii)* achieve decentralized development in small towns and villages; *(iv)* develop sub-contracting relationship with large industries; *(v)* establish common facility Service Centers, etc.

This was a centrally sponsored programme till 1979. Thereafter, it was transferred to the State Industrial Development Corporations (SIDCs). This encouraged, the Stage Government, to continue with the development of Industrial Estates/Areas through the SIDCs.

Additional facilities were extended by the different States to entrepreneurs who were setting up new units as well as to those units which were moving out of non-conforming areas and relocating to the developed IEs/ Areas. These facilities included subsidy on rent for factory accommodation, allotment of sheds on hire purchase as well as outright sale. Other incentives like concessional charges for water and power, exemption form Sales Tax and Octroi (building material, transport subsidy, etc.) were also offered.

EPZs/SEZs Export Industrial Parks

Special incentives for firms, small or large, to undertake manufacturing of export items for export from India have been provided by the Government of India through the establishment of Export Processing Zones (EPZs), recently modified as Special Economic Zones (SEZs) or through 100 per cent export-oriented units (EOUs) set up outside of such zones.

There are also several Technology Parks with focus on specific industries, like the Electronics Hardware Technology Parks (EPZs), Software Technology Parks (STPs), Bio-Tech Park, Leather Park, etc. with specialized infrastructure, technology back-up and escort services.

Integrated Infrastructural Development Scheme (IID)

Consequent to policy measures for the promotion and strengthening of small and tiny village enterprises announced on 6 August, 1991, the scheme of Integrated Infrastructural Development (IID) (including technological back-up services) in rural/backward areas was announced by the Government of India on 7 March 1994.

The Scheme aimed at augmenting infrastructural facilities in the rural and backward areas with a special emphasis on the linkage between agriculture and industry. The scheme covered centrally developed backward districts other than those covered under the Growth Centre Scheme.

The Objectives of the IID Scheme were: 1. To establish approximately 50 IID centers in rural areas/backward districts in the country; 2. To promote SSI and tiny unit clusters with a view to the creation of employment opportunities ad to develop exports, 3. To promote stronger linkages between agriculture' and industry, 4. To Provide Common Service facilities and technological back up services in selected Centres, and, 5. To create/upgrade infrastructure facilities like power, water, tele-communication etc. in new/existing Centres/Industrial Areas.

Institutional Support to Small Enterprises in India

There is a network of organizations to support the development of the VSIs. The Small Scale Industries Board is an apex advisory body constituted by the Government of India to render advice on all the issues pertaining to the SSI sector. The Board was constituted in 1954 to facilitate co-ordination and provide Inter-institutional linkages for the development of the sector. The Union Industries Minister is the Chairman of the Board which consists of State Industries Ministers, select members of Parliament, Secretaries of various departments of central Government. Heads of financial institutions, industries associations and eminent experts in the SSI field.

The Department of SSI and Agro & Rural Industries (SSI and A & ARI) was created under the Union Ministry of Industry to formulate policy framework and initiate appropriate programmes and schemes for the promotion of SSIs in the country.

The range of functions of the department include the setting up of a network of institutions to render services of a varied nature like, techno-economic and managerial aspects, training, testing facilities, marketing assistance, etc. these activities are supported by a host of other Central/State Departments. Agencies, and Autonomous Institutions all over the country.

The office of the Development (Commissioner Small Scale Industries), known as the Small Industries Development Organisation (SIDO) was set up in 1951 is the nodal agency for implementation of Central Government policies and plays a constructive role in the strengthening of the SSI sector.

The SIDO functions through a network of Small Industry Service Institutes (SISIs) and a host of other field centers, the major SSI-related activities of SIDO include evolving all India policies and programmes, co-ordinating policies and programmes of State Governments, liaisoning with different State and Central Ministries, Planning Commission, RBI and Financial Institutions. SIDO also provides a comprehensive range of extension services through allied institutions and monitors Government-sponsored programmes.

At the State level, the Commissioner/Directorate of Industries implement policies for the promotion d development of small scale, cottage, medium and large-scale industries. The Central policies for the SSI sector serve as the guidelines, but each State evolves its own policy and package of incentives.

The State departments also oversee activities of the field offices, viz., District Industries Centres (DICs), etc. In addition, State Financial Corporations, State Small Industries Development to assist the promotion ad development of SSIs. Other regional level agencies include State Infrastructure Development Corporations, State Co-operative Banks, Regional Rural Banks, State Export Corporations, Agro Industries Corporation and Handloom and Handicrafts Corporations. For the purpose of human resources development, there is a network of specialized institutes associated with SIDO. At grassroots level, NGOs play important role for the development of tiny units.

Industry Associations provide support to the SSI sector and offer with a common platform to raise industry-related issues. Government policies, in recent years, have stressed the increasing role of Industry Associations in the setting up of common facilities and other ventures in the area of technology, marketing and other support services.

Women Entrepreneurs

The importance of the economic development of women takes on an added dimension in India when considered in the context of the prevailing social, legal and economic norms. The government has, therefore, taken several steps to promote women entrepreneurship.

In view of the initiative shown by women in various economic activities, promotional organizations have been organizing special programmes for them. This trend indicates a shift towards a gender-specific approach to such programmes in order to enhance the competence of women in order to enhance the competence of women in the establishment and management of SSIs.

The 1991 Industrial Policy has envisaged special training programmes to support women entrepreneurs. Accordingly, women entrepreneurs are receiving training through Entrepreneurship Development Progrmmes (EDPs) conducted by various institutions and organisations both at the Central and State levels.

The SIDO, with its field offices all over the country, has been carrying out development programmes for women entrepreneurs and is providing technical schemes for the setting up of SSI units. In view of changing outlook of the promotion of women enterprises, the SSI Board in 1991 revised the definition of women enterprises by omitting the condition of employing 50 per cent of women workers. This provided a boost to women entrepreneurs to take up businesses and avail of facilities/concessions as are applicable to all SSIs.

The SIDBI, has instituted various developmental initiatives towards promoting women enterprises. The Bank has designed programmes, with a focus on women, viz. Mahila Vikas Nidhi, Mahila Udyam Nidhi, Micro Credit

Scheme, Women Entrepreneurship Development Programmes, etc. These programmes have been formulated with the twin objectives of: *(i)* providing training and extension services support to women entrepreneurs through a comprehensive package suited to their skills and socio-economic status; and *(ii)* extending financial assistance on liberal terms, to enable them to set up industrial units. In the small-scale sector.

Andhra Pradesh has set up an exclusive Industrial Estate For Women Entrepreneurs.

Marketing

Marketing is a major problem area of the VSI sector. This sector generally experiences a lack of resources for sales promotion and advertising. Institutional assistance, therefore, is, often, very much essential for marketing of SSI products.

The marketing infrastructure, as available for SSIs consists of a combination of agencies and inventive schemes such as those mentioned below.

1. *NSIC:* Registers SSI and tiny units under a single point registration and secures orders for the supply of various stores, on preferential terms tendered by the DGS&D.
2. *Sub-Contracting Exchanges:* There are 16 such exchanges that operate through the Small Industries Service Institutes (SISIs). These exchanges enlist SSIs and identify items for ancillarisation from various Public Sector Undertakings. These offices promote contacts between large and medium scale industries on the one hand and SSI ancillary units on thee other to secure sub-contracting jobs.
3. *Quality Certification: (a)* The Bureau of Indian Standards (BIS) sets the standards for different manufactured products and it registers SSIs for the-adoption of quality standards as a measure of

marketing support. *(b)* SIDO has set up 4 Regional Testing Centres, which provide testing facilities to SSI units as per BIS standards. In addition, there are a number of field-testing stations extending testing facilities and assistance to SSIs. *(c)* SIDO is operating a scheme to reimburse (upto 75 per cent subject to a maximum of Rs. 0.075 million) the cost of acquiring ISO 9000 certification.

4. *Marketing Development Assistance (MDA) Scheme:* Ministry of Commerce, Government of India reimburses the expenditure incurred by the SSI delegations that visit foreign countries (60) per cent of the expenditure incurred by the delegation) for the purpose of exploring marketing possibilities. This incentive is extended to admissible items only.
5. *Training Programmes for Export Packaging:* SIDO, in partnership with the Indian Institute of Packaging organizes training programmes for SSI exporters on packaging for exports. Exporters are provided information on the latest packaging standards and techniques in order to boost exports.
6. *Organising Exhibitions and International Trade Fair:* For promoting exports, STDO annually participates in selected international Trade Fair and Exhibitions held abroad by the India Trade Promotion Organisation (ITPO) All expenses on space hiring, display, shipment, insurance, handling and clearance, publicity etc. are borne by SIDO.
7. *Export Promotion Councils:* The existence of export promotion councils for specific industries provides the SSI member units with platform for export marketing. A number of Export Promotion Councils are providing marketing infrastructure through procurement of direct orders and distribution of items among member units for production and sale.

   The Councils also arrange for quality testing of

products, pre-shipment inspection, packaging and sales transactions assistance. These bodies arrange for the participation of member units in various Exhibitions and Trade Fairs.

8. *SIDBI's Marketing Finance & Development Department:* SIDBI established its Marketing Finance and Development Department (MFDD) in January 1996 to focus attention on marketing-related activities undertaken by the SSI sector. The Bank formulated a comprehensive scheme for providing financial assistance to SSIs enabling them to undertake various marketing activities as also to assist institutions/agencies engaged in strengthening the existing marketing channels and infrastructure for the SSI sector. A special Marketing Assistance Development Fund with sub-allocation for women entrepreneurs has been set up. A number of development and support services have also been undertaken by the Department to assist the marketing efforts of the SSI units.

State Industrial Policies

The State/UT Government pursue the Central Government industrial policies and assistance is obtained under different centrally sponsored schemes/incentives for disbursement among eligible SSIs. This Central policy frame work serves as a guiding principle for States, which evolve respective Governments also design suitable incentives to encourage existing units to expand/diversity products and support entrepreneurs to establish new units.

In this context, State Governments provide technical and other support services to SSIs through the Directorate of Industries and DICs. The main areas of support and facilities are listed below.

1. To develop and manage industrial areas by respective Industrial Development and investment Corporation.

2. Financial support services by State financial Corporations (SFCs).
3. Technical guidance by Technical Consultancy Organisation (TCOs).
4. Human resources development by a host of training institutions.
5. Infrastructure development by Infrastructural Development Corporations.
6. Export promotion by Small Industry and Export Corporations.
7. Single Window Assistance by District Industries Centres.

Conclusion

Besides above, State Governments also offer a range of incentive measures for providing an impetus to industrialization. These incentives to SSIs are mainly by way of providing land and developed plots/sheds on concessional terms, industrial infrastructural facilities, subsidy on investment (in selected areas) and on generating sets, sales tax and stamp duty exemptions, water supply at reduced rates, seed capital assistance for setting up of units etc.

MISD also organized a two-day workshop on PIMS and computer related issues. This workshop apprise the participant for closing the old files. To upgrade the skills of staff, an interactive in–house training of office automation and LAN was organized for the staff of the Council.

7

Floricultural Development Under Gobalization

Introduction

After liberalization (1991), the Government of India identified floriculture as a sunrise industry and realized the need to augment the existing infrastructure facilities within the country to garner the significant share of global trade in flowers. A number of infrastructure projects especially cold chain infrastructure were commissioned and completed. The Central as well as State Governments has given a package of incentives and concessions to the floriculture industry. The following are the policy changes made after the pursuit of liberalization policy:

(a) The quarantine procedures have been simplified and made easy for the import of seeds and plating materials.

(b) Import duty on floriculture planting material has bee reduced from 55 per cent to 10 per cent.

(c) Import duty on specified goods for greenhouse has been brought down from 136 per cent to 25 per cent.

(d) Import duty on precooling units and refrigerated transport units has been reduced to 25 per cent.

(e) Import permits for flower, seeds and tissue culture materials of plant origin have been waived.

(f) Floriculture units can avail the benefits of duty free imports if they export 50 per cent of their production.

(g) Setting up walk in type cold storage has been allowed at international airports for export of export consignments.

A centrally sponsored scheme on commercial floriculture was launched for the first time during the 8th five-year plan with the objective of improving supply of quality planting materials and technology transfer through demonstration and training with an outlay of Rs. 14.29 crores. The total allocation available to floriculture scheme for the 9th five-year plan period was Rs. 19.90 crores, and increase of 39 per cent over the 8th five-year plan period.

Trends in India's Floriculture Exports

The modern floriculture industry is still in its infancy and the country took the first step towards the export-oriented floriculture in 1993 with the exchange of delegations with the world leader-the Netherlands. India's rich heritage of plant genera owes much to its diverse topograph and climatic conditions which have contributed much to the growth of this industry.

With the changing life styles and increased urban affluence, floriculture products have assumed a commercial status. In the past three or four decades appreciation of the potential of commercial floriculture has resulted in the blossoming of the sector into a viable agri-business option. In recent years, India has emerged as one of leading growers of cut flowers entering to markets around the world. India's late entry into floriculture (compared to countries like Columbia and Kenya) gave her the advantage of a quick learning curve and therefore early adoption of the latest technologies. Consequently, Indian projects today include traditional greenhouse cultivation, modern climatically controlled and automated systems as well as the latest methods in hydroponics.

From a modest 10 hectare in 1993, the green house area under cut flowers has grown to over 200 hectares. More than 70 units are producing cut flowers under green houses for export. It is estimated that more than Rs. 4 billion investment has already been made in the sector in the past five years. During the last five years, India's floriculture export has increased 25 times. Bangalore, Pune, Hyderabad, Thiruvanthapuram, Gurgaon in Haryana and Delhi are the major centers of floriculture Industry.

On the above background, the aim of the paper is to examine the trends in floriculture exports of the country over a period 1990-1998. Accordingly an analysis is made with the help of secondary data collected from Agricultural and Processed Food Product Development Authority (APEDA).

Table 1: India's Export of Floriculture Products (Value in Rs. Lakhs)

Year	*Value*	*% Change in 5 Years*	*Annual % Change*
1989-90	675.00		-
1990-91	786.00		16
1991-92	1480.00		88
1992-93	1491.00		07
1993-94	1884.00	179	26
1994-95	3084.0		64
1995-96	6041.00		95
1996-97	6340.00		05
1997-98	8121.00		28
1998-99	9661.00	213	19

Source: Computed from DGCIS, Annual Volume & Export State for Agro & Food Products India 1995-96 & 1998-99 APEDA, Delhi, India.

It is evident from the Table 1 that the earning from flower exports in 1989-90 was just Rs. 675 lakhs, which shot up to Rs. 1884 lakhs in 1993-94. The result shows that during the five years period from (1989-90 to 1993-94), floriculture industry witnessed a remarkable growth of 179 per cent. During 1995-96 the country earned Rs. 6014 lakhs as against Rs. 3084 lakhs during the previous year witnessing almost a two fold increase. In 1996-97, India could cash Rs. 6340 lakhs by way of floriculture exports. In terms of growth rate, there was slow down during this period, as industry grew only at 5 per cent rate. However, the industry picked up afterwards and in 1997-98 the value of floriculture exports was Rs. 8121 lakhs which has increased to Rs. 9661 lakhs in 1998-99. Further, it is evident that during the five years period (1994-95 to 1998-99) the exports of floriculture from India registered a remarkable growth of 213 per cent.

When we consider the growth rate of floriculture exports for the last 10 years (1990-99), the growth was really fantastic at 13.31 per cent. It shows that floriculture products among many agricultural exports took a lead. Even overall agricultural exports got boosted merely due to presence of exports of this sector. Among various flowers it is red rose cut flowers, which accounts for more than 60 per cent of exports of floriculture products. Thus the growth of floriculture industry in India is rightly called as "RED REVOLUTION".

In order to sharpen the results the annual growth rate of export value was worked out in Table 2 for the period of ten years. The annual growth rate of floriculture exports was the highest at 19.6 per cent in 1995-96 followed by 16.4 per cent in 1994-95 and it has always remained above 10 per cent in other years. On an average the growth in floriculture exports was around 13 per cent per annum during the ten years period (1990-99). This indicates that the growth rate of export value of floriculture is substantially high and it is concluded that impetus given by the central government in this direction yielded results and further efforts are to be supplemented by the state governments since the agriculture comes under state list.

Table 2: Percentage Change Rate of Floriculture Exports from India Over a Period 1990-99

(Value in Lakh Rs)

Year	*Value of Export*	*Percentage Change over Previous year*
1989-90	675.00	
1990-91	786.00	11.6
1991-92	1480.00	18.8
1992-93	1491.00	10.1
1993-94	1884.00	12.6
1994-95	3084.0	16.4
1995-96	6041.00	19.6
1996-97	6340.00	10.5
1997-98	8121.00	12.8
1998-99	9661.00	11.9

Source: Computed from APEDA op. cit.

Composition of Floriculture Products

Floriculture exports from India include bulbs, tubers, tuberous roots, cut flowers for bouquets, foliages, flowering plants and other live plants. Traditionally the business of floriculture was mainly in bulbs, flower plants and foliage. The consumption of cut flowers with long stems is of comparatively recent origin, but it is the fastest growing segment now. The detailed analyses about different variety of flowers have been discussed below:

Table 3: Variety of Floriculture Products Exported from India During 1993-94 to 1998-99 (Rs. Lakhs)

Product	*93-94*	*94-95*	*95-96*	*96-97*	*97-98*	*98-99*	*% change in 98-99 over 93-94*
Bulbs, tubers	111.45	16.02	52.45	89.66	248.87	68.45	-38.58
Tuberous roots	(5.9)	(0.5)	(0.9)	(1.4)	(3.1)	(0.7)	
Bulbs Horticultural	14.29	53.68	75.84	10.49	39.25	27.14	89.92
	(0.8)	(1.3)	(1.3)	(0.2)	(0.5)	(0.3)	
Chicory plants	0.96	4.26	-	-	-	0.17	-
Other bulbs/tubers	22.82	44.38	63.86	28.26	9.95	15.12	-33.74
	(1.3)	(1.4)	(1.1)	(0.4)		(0.2)	
Unrooted cuttings	37.24	271.35	220.4	58.22	31.23	49.06	31.74
	(2.0)	(8.8)	(3.7)	(0.9)	(0.4)	(0.5)	
Edible fruit tree/ Grafted or not	1.48	1.24	1.73	2.29	-	-	-
Cactus	-	0.03	2.56	1.00	0.95	3.31	-
Rhododendrons Grafted or not	-	-	0.93	3.12	28.7	-	-
Roses Grafted or not	5.66	28.89	129.08	87.88	81.98	63.95	1029.86
	(0.3)	(0.9)	(2.1)	(1.4)	(1.0)	(0.7)	
Live mushrooms spawn	9.79	-	2.09	-	-	-	-
Flowering plants	35.37	53.46	66.41	14.17	-	-	-
	(1.9)	(1.7)	(1.1)	(0.2)			
Other live plants	208.81	224.75	372.08	97.6	-	-	-
	(11.1)	(7.3)	(6.2)	(1.5)			
Cut flowers for	99.64	299.81	1003.3	1808.6	1894.12	2511.66	2420.73
Bouquets /fresh	(58)	(9.7)	(16.7)	(28.5)	(23.3)	(26)	
Other cut flowers	1092	1958	3645.6	3233.9	5327.29	5104.01	367.35
for Bouquets fresh	(5.3)	(63.5)	(61.0)	(51)	(65.6)	(53)	
Other foliages/buds for bouquets fresh	6.77	24.59	19.52	0.53	0.33	-	-
Foliages/branches/	237.2	103.48	358.3	256.2	483.54	1816.51	665.81

Buds not fresh	(12.6)	(3.4)	(5.9)	(4.04)	(5.9)	(19)	
Total flori. Exports	1884	3084	6014	6340	8121	9661	412.88

Source: APEDA, New Delhi.

Note: Figures in parentheses indicate percentage to total.

Among the different floriculture products, that India has been exporting, (Table 3) the percentage share of bulbs, tubers, tuberous roots has declined. Bulbs, tubers and tuberous roots are the products that may be planted in pots, boxes or similar containers. These items are demanded in Japan, Netherlands, Germany and USA. These four countries together buy more than 78 per cent of the bulbs, tubers, and tuberous roots exports from India. Japan alone imported 30 per cent of these items exported from India in 1998-99 as against 12 per cent during the previous year. Netherlands' import of these items from India was 22 per cent during 1998-99 as compared to 36 per cent previous year. Another buyer of these items is Germany which imported 16 per cent of these items during 1998-99. In all India has earned Rs. 6.84 crores from these items in 1998-99.

Live plants both flowering and other have disappeared from our export basket from 1997-98, which had claimed 13 per cent share in the total floriculture exports during 1993-94. Live plants are used for permanent and semi permanent decoration in offices and homes. These are whole plants, which are suitable for planting for ornamental purposes. Ornamental plants include flowers, bulbs, corms and tubers in the dormant as well as growth and blossoming stage and other live plants such as young vegetable plants, mushroom spawn which cannot always be separated from ornamental plants.

However, the share of fresh cut flowers in the total has increased continuously and rapidly from 5.3 per cent in 1993-94 to 16.7 per cent in 1995-96 and further to 28.5 per cent in 1996-97 (but witnessed a sharp fall to 23 per cent in 1997-98) However, this item has picked up and its share in the total floriculture products had increased to 26 per cent in 1998-99. Cut flowers with a suitable stems of varying length make them suitable for bouquets or for ornamental purposes. Cut flowers generally mean all cut plant components and the economic value of which lies in the decorative effects of their blossoms, roses, carnations, chrysanthemum, orchids, gladioli etc. come under the category of cut flowers. The most colourful varieties of cut flowers are available in carnation than other cut flowers. It is the second largest export potential cut flower next to roses, which can be grown in any adverse climatic condition under protected cultivation. These cut flowers for bouquets/fresh have high demand in Japanese market. Japan alone bought 33 per cent of total cut flower exported from India during 1998-99. Netherlands, imported 19 per cent, Singapore and USA's shares are 6.5 and 6 per cent in the total cut flower exports respectively, Germany, U.K., Australia, UAE, Switzerland are the other major importers of our cut flowers. Total export earnings from cut flowers in 1997-98 was Rs. 18.94 crores which has increased to Rs. 25.11 crores in 1998-99. The fresh cut flower exports over a period (1994-99) reveals that it is Japan whose consumption of Indian flowers is highest (Rs. 2649 lakhs) followed by Netherlands (Rs. 1821 lakhs).

Cut foliage refers to plant parts namely leaves, twigs, grasses, shoots etc. the economic value of which lies not in the decorative effect of the blossoms but in its colour and shape. Fresh cut foliage is used in combination with cut flowers for bouquets, flower arrangements and decorations when cut flowers and foliage are presented together in pre-arranged bunch.

The share of other (dry) cut flowers has shown violent fluctuations. It was 58 per cent in 1993-94 and has increased to 63.5 per cent in 1994-95 and declined to 51 pre cent in 1996-97 and once again increased to 65.6 per cent in 1997-98 However, in 1998-99 its share has come down to 53 per cent. (Table 4). Today, India is the leading exporter of dry flowers to the world's leading markets; Europe and U.S.A. During 1998-99 USA imported 25 per cent of the total flowers from India as against 31 per cent during the previous year, while Netherlands bought 19 per cent as against 21 per cent during the previous year. During the year 1998-99 Germany imported 12 per cent, U.K. over 5 per cent of the total dry flowers from India (Table 5) USA, Netherlands, Germany, Japan and UK together purchased about 72 per cent of dry flowers exported from India. Japan has been proving as a potential market for Indian dry flowers. During 1998-99 Japan has bought 11 per cent of the dry cut flowers of India as against just 2 per cent during the previous year. Certainly, the Indian dry flower market has found its way to Japanese households. Another potential market for Indian dry cut flowers is Denmark which has bought flowers worth Rs. 1.8 crores during 1998-99 (3.5 per cent). Other major importers of dry flowers are Italy, France, Spain, etc. Total export earnings from this during 1998-99 was Rs. 51.04 crores which was lower the previous year (Rs. 53.27 crores).

Table 4: Export of Fresh Cut Flowers from India to Different Countries (Value in Rs. Lakhs)

Countries	93-94	94-95	95-96	96-97	97-98	98-99	Total in 6 years	% Share
U.S.A	392.12	777.14	1401.59	1064.72	1646.22	1274.07	6556.16	32.2
Netherlands	0.6	199.40	512.70	468.64	1113.75	967.55	3262.64	16.02
Germany	173.31	344.43	560.00	692.16	847.9	616.36	3234.16	15.88
U.K.	74.21	217.08	362.10	265.29	459.55	268.59	1646.82	8.09
Italy	67.54	166.98	130.40	131.61	274.58	207.33	978.44	4.80
France	23.22	38.42	54.88	86.17	174.4	180.37	557.46	2.74
Spain	6.1	5.09	65.89	25.46	141.16	107.69	351.39	1.73
Japan	5.5	37.82	171.20	166.15	109.52	603.11	1093.3	5.4
Australia	14.86	18.50	35.25	41.1	89.27	58.68	257.66	1.27
Belgium	2.87	4.25	27.39	25.15	88.36	38.73	186.75	0.92
Sri Lanka	19.72	40.87	81.51	77.9	53.4	7.63	281.03	1.38
Singapore	0.05	4.05	3.34	7.46	49.07	106.38	170.35	0.84
U.A.E	2.77	8.27	8.48	6.19	32.61	40.48	98.8	0.5
China	4.35	1.83	-	0.5	30.87	5.3	42.85	0.2
Hong Kong	0.75	8.07	10.4	32.76	30.03	25.08	107.09	0.5
Israel	2.44	6.33	13.83	16.50	23.45	10.24	72.79	0.4
Chinese Taipei	-	1.78	24.38	6.96	19.24	4.47	56.83	0.3
Canada	4.35	3.19	20.55	9.59	14.39	14.35	66.42	0.3
Switzerland	0.51	1.56	2.80	0.99	14.38	7.63	27.87	0.14
Saudi Arabia	35.73	26.13	45.37	23.56	13.35	26.83	170.97	0.8
Others	261.12	46.31	113.50	85.04	101.79	533.15	1140.91	5.6
Total	1092.12	1957.8	3645.56	3233.90	5327.29	5104.02	20360.69	100.0

The demand for dry flowers is mainly due to the increased interest of the discerning buyers in Indian dry flower and arrangement for their supply. The dry flower is lucrative for the traders because of its long lasting property and its increasing demand in the world market.

The growing awareness for dry flowers in India is evident through the increasing demand (even) in the domestic the year in the leading flower shops along with the cut flowers. The prices for the dry flowers vary from Rs. 5/- for a flower stem to anything above Rs. 500/- for exotic arrangement. The availability of cheap labour due to burgeoning population enables the Indian exporters to pack their products with more man hours fetching more profit.

Table 5: Export of Fresh Cut Flowers from India to Different Countries (Value in Rs. Lakhs)

Countries	*93-94*	*94-95*	*95-96*	*96-97*	*97-98*	*98-99*	*Total in 6 years*	*% Share*
Japan	3.22	82.55	359.32	699.8	670.55	833.90	2649.34	34.5
Netherlands	10.04	91.02	247.99	502.02	491.74	478.45	1821.26	23.72
USA	11.75	24.95	176.52	131.11	127.83	145.90	618.06	8.05
Singapore	0.78	4.37	11.9	46.56	115.84	163.64	343.09	4.5
Germany	9.57	25.38	92.56	127.68	99.62	138.44	493.25	6.42
U.K	14.2	11.13	33.45	149.3	97.14	139.73	444.95	5.8
Australia	-	0.005	1.32	8.61	68.72	152.17	230.83	3.0
U.A.E.	21.2	33.88	24.59	42.91	59.41	99.88	281.87	3.67
France	0.18	-	-	10.44	32.66	12.29	55.57	0.7
Switzerland	1.37	2.58	2.42	7.85	26.03	64.15	105.39	1.37
Italy	2.10	1.64	22.0	8.56	16.98	46.58	97.81	1.27
Malaysia	0.21	0.26	-	3.83	11.35	14.67	30.32	0.39
Chinese Taipei	-	-	-	5.73	7.38	1.74	14.85	0.2
Saudi Arabia	4.14	1.69	2.72	4.91	7.16	20.96	41.58	0.54
Pakistan	-	-	0.59	-	6.18	1.33	8.1	0.1
Hong Kong	7.3	9.03	15.04	10.74	6.11	27.0	75.22	0.98
Spain	-	4.49	-	0.63	5.43	5.43	15.98	0.21
Others	13.58	68.35	12.87	47.97	44.04	164.41	351.22	4.57
Total	86.06	299.81	1003.29	1808.65	894.12	2511.66	7679.69	100.00

Source: Computed from export Statistics for Agro & Food Products India 1994-95 & 1997-98, APEDA, New Delhi, India.

Dry flowers dried, preserved and processed have an upper hand over the cut and fresh flowers as they are near to the natural and have an everlasting colour. They are like mummies without any preservatives. Whereas the fresh flowers though exquisite in their beauty are expensive, short lived and available only during a particular season. The dry flower can withstand the heat of summer and cold of winter, the dry flower have been put to many beautiful and varied uses. Apart from bouquets and flower arrangements their flexibility enables them to be put to a variety of artistic uses to make long lasting pictures, flower balls, cards, covers, pomanders sweet smelling pot-purri and many more things. The dry flower has a large potential in the Indian market as compared to silk and synthetic flowers as they are cheaper, available in a varied range to choose from, eco-friendly and bio-degradable and are easily got throughout the year.

The share of dry foliages/branches/ buds has fluctuated during the five years period. This item shared more than 12 per cent in 1995-96 and recovered a little to 5.9 per cent in 1997-98. However, its share has increased to 19 per cent by improving its exports from Rs 4.8 crores in 1997-98 Rs 18.16 crores during the year 1998-99. (Table 5). Dry foliages/branches/buds exported by U.S.A., Germany, U.K. Netherlands, Italy etc. In 1997-98 U.S.A. alone imported 35 per cent of the total dry foliages/ branches/buds exported from India and this increased to 43 per cent in 1998-99. The share of Germany, U.K., Italy, Netherlands were 19 per cent, 10 per cent and 8 per cent respectively during the year 1997-98 and this share has changed to 12 per cent, 10 per cent, 7 per cent respectively for the year 1998-99. For this item also Denmark emerged as a new market with its share of 6 per cent during the year 1998-99.

(1) The three items namely fresh cut flowers, other than fresh cut flowers and foliages/branches/buds [not fresh] accounted for 74 per cent of the total Indian

floriculture exports in 1993-94 and their share has increased to 83 per cent in 1995-96 and 94.8 per cent in 1997-98 and further to 98 per cent in 1998-99. (2) Over a period (1994-99) 99 products like bulbs, tubers, tuberous roots, bulbs horticulture, unrooted, cutting etc. Have shown a declining trend. Some of the items like edible fruit tree/grafted or not, Rhododendrons grafted or not live mushrooms spawn, flowering plants and other and live plants have disappeared from our export basket during the recent years. (3) Cut flowers for bouquets both fresh and others, and foliages/ branches/buds not fresh have witnessed a remarked growth over a period (1994-99).

Direction of Trade

The world consumption of floriculture is approximately Rs. 70,000 crores; cut flowers contribute nearly 60 per cent. Consumption of cut flowers worldwide has risen by 11 per cent since 1985. It is however concentrated only in three regions, Western Europe, North America and Japan. The industry is growing at a rate of 12-15 per cent annually.

Indian flowers are now well received in all the major auctions and direct markets of the world. This includes Europe, North America, the Middle East, South East Asia, Australia and Japan.

USA is the largest imported of Indian floriculture products. In 1994-95 USA purchased Rs. 953.27 lakhs worth flower projects from India. This constituted about 31 per cent of the total floriculture products exported from India. In 1996-97 USA imported 27.7 per cent of Indian flower Products valuing about Rs. 1758 lakhs. This has been lower than the previous year both in absolute (Rs. 1778 lakhs in 1995-96) and relative (29.5 per cent) terms. In 1997-98 USA bought floriculture products worth Rs. 1979 lakhs from India which increased further to Rs. 2222 lakhs in 1998-99. But its share in the total Indian floriculture exports has declined further from 24 per cent decline is the high quality consciousness of the Americans.

Table 6: Country wise Export of Floriculture Products from India over a Period 1994-99

(Value in Rs. Lakhs)

Countries	*93-94*	*94-95*	*95-96*	*96-97*	*97-98*	*98-99*	*% change in 97-98 over 93-94*
U.S.A	516.09	953.27	1778.05	1758.22	1979.2	2222.64	330.67
Netherlands	167.53	463.84	1263.62	1240.75	1773.51	1645.20	882.03
Germany	250.38	405.13	774.74	932.26	1044.56	983.33	392.73
Japan	36.42	134.29	609.4	916.28	831.13	1501.02	4021.42
U.K.	257.07	421.78	532.59	439.54	657.43	591.59	130.13
Italy	87.57	181.2	208.15	168.76	356.37	383.07	337.44
France	40.49	54.84	84.22	129.65	212.34	250.30	518.17
Australia	16.09	18.97	42.05	61.3	175.53	219.60	1264.82
Singapore	2.90	8.59	15.85	70.56	172.93	282.14	9628.96
Spain	8.25	9.59	65.97	31.36	155.57	155.24	1781.69
Belgium	12.06	29.53	36.94	36.02	122.81	157.75	1208.04
U.A.E	57.21	105.49	71.19	71.49	110.77	147.21	157.31
Yemen Republic	6.26	2.94	-	8.11	62.82	63.20	909.58
Sri Lanka	24.31	65.81	90.5	86.02	59.16	105.42	333.65
Switzerland	2.82	4.15	8.78	16.13	42.88	72.78	2480.85
Others	398.2	223.38	432.1	373.41	363.66	880.48	121.11
Total	1883.65	3083.38	6014.15	6339.86	8120.67	9660.97	412.88

Source: Computed from Export Statistics for Agro & Food Products India 1994-95 & 1997-98, APEDA, New Delhi, India.

Table 7: Country wise Export of Floriculture Products from India over a Period 1994-99

(Value in Rs. Lakhs)

Countries	*1993-94*	*1994-95*	*1995-96*	*1996-97*	*1997-98*	*1998-99*
U.S.A	27.40	30.91	29.56	27.73	24.37	23.0
Netherlands	8.89	15.04	21.01	19.57	21.84	17.03
Germany	13.29	13.14	12.88	14.70	12.86	10.18
Japan	1.93	4.35	10.13	14.45	10.23	15.54
U.K.	13.65	13.68	8.85	6.93	8.09	6.12
Italy	4.65	5.88	3.46	2.66	4.38	3.96
France	2.15	1.78	1.40	2.04	2.61	2.60
Australia	0.85	0.62	0.70	0.96	2.16	2.27
Singapore	0.15	0.28	0.26	1.11	2.13	2.92
Spain	0.44	0.31	1.09	0.49	1.92	1.62
Belgium	0.64	0.96	0.61	0.57	1.51	1.63
U.A.E.	3.04	3.42	1.18	1.13	1.36	1.52
Yemen Republic	0.33	3.10	-	1.13	1.36	1.52
Sri Lanka	1.29	2.13	1.50	1.36	0.73	1.09
Switzerland	0.15	0.13	0.15	0.25	0.53	0.75
Others	21.15	7.27	7.22	5.92	4.51	9.12
Total	100.00	100.00	100.00	100.00	100.00	100.00

Source: Computed from Export Statistics for Agro & Food Products India 1994-95 & 1997-98, APEDA, New Delhi, India.

Next major importer of flower products from India is the Netherlands the world leader in floriculture industry. Netherlands' share in India's total flower exports has continuously and steadily increased from 9 per cent in 1993-94 to 22 per cent in 1997-98 but declined to 17 per cent during 1998-99. Even in absolute terms Netherlands import of floriculture products from India has declined from Rs. 1773.57 lakhs in 1997-98 to Rs. 1645 lakhs during 1998-99. This decline may be attributed to the fact that Indian firms are exploring new markets for direct sale rather than auction sale at Netherlands.

Germany buys a considerable amount of floriculture items from India. Germany is another important market for Indian flowers. Germany has been importing more or less a constant amount of flowers from India hovering around 13-15 per cent of total Indian flower exports during the period from 1993-94 to 1997-98 Germany has imported flower products worth Rs. 1045 lakhs from India which however has declined to Rs. 983 lakhs in 1998-99. As a result its share in the total Indian flower exports has come down from 13 per cent in 1997-98 to 10 per cent during the year 1998-99.

Japan is another important market for Indian flowers. The flower export to Japanese market has green many fold over the period (1994-99). In fact during the year 1998-99 Japan occupied the position of third major importer of Indian flowers. In 1993-94 Japan imported flowers worth Rs. 36.42 lakhs which constituted less than 2 per cent of the total floriculture exports from India. But in later years Japan has started buying more and more floriculture products form India and its share has continuously increased from mere 2 per cent in 1996-97. However, Japan's import of floriculture items from India has declined to Rs. 831.13 lakhs in 1997-98 from Rs. 916.28 lakhs in 1996-97, which has constituted 10 per cent of the total floriculture export from India. However, during the year 1998-99 Japan imported flowers worth Rs. 1501.02 lakhs and its share has sharply increased to 15.54 per cent in the total and pushed Germany to fourth position and became the third largest buyer of Indian flowers. Consequently most of the projects are gearing up to specific tastes and preferences of the Japanese buyers and trying to strengthen the trade with Japan. Japan is closer to India in terms of distance as well culture. Both these factors are important in business. Accordingly firms are concentrating more on pastel colours, newer varieties, minimum stem length of 50 cm and most importantly a longer vase life. Such an orientation along with a substantially improved logistics including cold chain maintenance through the newly constructed cold stores at airports and round the year production give India an edge over its competitors.

Thus the prominent countries which have high potential for Indian flowers are Japan, Singapore, Australia, Belgium, Switzerland and Yemen Republic. It is evident from the Table 6 that the exports growth rate from India to these countries have exceeded over a period of 6 years (1994-99). Thus it is concluded that Indian floriculture has not only diversified but also changed its direction from USA, Netherlands, Germany party towards new green pastures.

Other promising markets for Indian floriculture are U.K. Italy, France, Australia, Singapore, Spain, Belgium and UAE. Another new market is Denmark which is emerging as a potential buyer of Indian flowers. Its import was negligible at Rs.1.57 lakhs during 1996-97 and Rs. 4.52 lakhs in 1997-98 but has increased to Rs. 313.07 lakhs during 1998-99 (3 per cent of the total flower exports from India). India has to carefully nurture such new markets. There is tremendous opportunity for exports. India can get good price provided it produces quality. This nascent industry can be a great foreign exchange earner, provide rural employment and contribute to women development. The market is big enough to take at least 100 times more than what we are producing at present, provided the present ills of the floriculture industry are cured by the government support as well as support from the Flower Grower's Associations.

8

Rural India—Cropping Patterns

Cropping activities go on all the year-round in India, provided water is available for crops. In northern India there are two distinct seasons Kharif (July to October) and Rabi (October to March) crops grown between March and June are known as said. In some parts of the country, there are no such distinct seasons but there they have their own classification of seasons. The villages revenue officials keep plot wise record of crops grown in each seasons. There are annually completed district wise, state wise and on all-India basis from there records are could calculate the relative abundance of a group of crops in a regions. These crops are grown sole or mixed (mixed cropping) or in a definite sequence (rotational cropping) the land may be occupied by one crop during one season (more cropping). The land may be occupied by one crop during one season (mono cropping) on by two crops (double–cropping) which may be grown in a year in sequence of late the trend is even towards more than two crops (multiple–cropping) in a year. These intensive cropping may be done either in sequence on even there may be relay–cropping one crop undersown in a standing crop. With wide-rowed slow–growing crops, companion crops may be grown. There are various ways of utilizing the land intensively. It is proposed to give a synoptic view of cropping patterns prevalent in the description of the factors that determine the cropping pattern a brief description of the factors that determine the cròpping system of an individual locality or region are briefly presented here.

In any locality the prevalent cropping systems are the cumulative results of past and present decisions are usually based on experience, tradition and political pressures and so on. Essentially they are answers to some of the following questions.

(a) What crops with the present pest–and–disease controls methods are ecologically practicable?

(b) What interactions occur among the ecologically practicable crops and the chosen crops and must be combined in a special way (rotations) farming systems

(c) Are any of the ecologically feasible crops ruled out by infrastructure factors

(d) Which of the crops now remaining on the list are more profitable

(e) What operational factors rule out or amend the size and method of any of the economically preferable crop combinations them of?

(f) Finally are the crop combinations the farming system and the input level suggested by this process of the individual farmers compatible with own skills enterprise preference, health age and capital?

The climate edaphic and socio–economic diversity of the Indian's crop–products scene in dotted with many. Cropping patterns with a geographical area of 328.048 million hectares, stretching between 8 degrees north and 36 degrees north latitude and between 68 degrees east and 98 degrees east longitude its attitude varying from the mean sea–level to the highest mountain ranges of the world, India presents a range and diversity of climate, flora and foam, with few parallels in the world. The country presents the paradox of containing in it the states with the highest mean annual rainfall in the world (Cherrapunji in Assam) and also dry semi–desert area in Rajasthan. The variability of rainfall is most important in all states, but especially where rainfall is low. In parts of Rajasthan and the Deccan the variability is more than 100 percent of the mean. Years of drought account for only to frequent a history of crop failures, where as the years of flood also cause very considerable loss of agricultural production. Temperatures also vary greatly, geographically and seasonally. Northern and central part of India in January have temperatures comparable with those in Europe in July, though with a greater daily range, but in these places in the premonsoon months the maximum temperature of over 40 degrees are reached over a large area. Frost may occur in winter even in the plains, as far south as a line drain through Bihar and Madhya Pradesh and may be heavy in Kashmir and areas north of Punjab.

Socio–economically, the peasantry ranges from the relatively affluent Punjab farmers who operate with a high input intensity in agriculture to the subsistent farmers of eastern and central India. They even today, sometimes various intensities of cultivation are practiced. The outstanding fact on the socio–economic front is the smallness of the holdings, the average farm size most of the areas being lower than that is inmost tropical country.

Crop production, therefore presents such as monsoons diversity owing to different in latitude, attitude and variability and variability of rainfall and edaphic diversity. The most important element of farming in India is the production of grains and the dominant food chain is grace man on this basis the country may be divided broadly into five agriculture regions.

(1) The rice region extends from the eastern part to include a very large part of the north–eastern and the south-eastern India, with another strip along the western coast.

(2) The wheat region, occupying most of the northern, western and central India.

(3) The millet–sorghum region, comprising Rajasthan, Madhya Pradesh and the Deccan plateau in the central of the Indian Peninsula.

(4) The temperate Himalayan region of Kashmir, Himachal Pradesh and Uttar Pradesh and some adjoining areas. Here, Potatoes are important as cereal crops (which are mainly maize and rice) and the tree fruits form a large part of agriculture production.

(5) The plantation–crops region of Assam and the hills of southern India where good–quality tea is produced. Then is an important production of high quality coffee in the hill of the western peninsular India. Rubber is mostly in Kerala. Several spices are also grown in Kerala and parts of Karnataka and Tamilnadu. There are some large estates, but most of the growers would come under the category of small holders. Sugarcane, which is many countries is a plantation crop, is almost entirely grown by small holders in India.

The Present Cropping Patterns

A broad picture of the major cropping patterns in India can be presented by taking the major crops into considerations. To began with the south–western monsoon crops (Kharif) bajra, maize, ragi, groundnut and cotton. Among the post monsoon crops (rabi) wheat, sorghum (rabi) and grains. Can also be considered to be approach the crop occupying the highest percentage of the shown or as the regions is taken as the base crop in the same season, are considered in the pattern. Also there crops . have been identified as associating themselves with a particular type of are grouped under one category. Similar requirement are grouped under one category. For example wheat, barley and oats, are taken as one category. Similarly the minor millets (paspalum, setaria and panicen spp) are grouped with sorghum or bajra certain other crops, such as the plantation crops and other industrial crops discussed separately.

The Kharif-Season Cropping Patterns

Among the kharif crops, rice, jowar, bajra, maize, groundnut and cotton are the prominent crops to be considered the base crops for describing the kahrif-cropping pattern.

The Rice-Based Croping Pattern

Rice is grown in the high rainfall area or in areas where supplemental irrigation is available to ensure good yields. If the crop has to depend solely on rainfall. It requires not less than 30 cm per month of rainfall over the entire growing period. However only 9 per cent of the area in the country comes under this category and it has in the eastern parts. Nearly 45 per cent of the total rice over in India recives.30cm per month of rainfall during the least two months (July–August) of the south western Monsoon and much less during other months. It contrast to there parts the eastern and southern regions comprising Assam, West Bengal, Coastal Orissa, Coastal Andhra Pradesh, Karnataka (most part). Tamilnadu and Kerala receive rainfall of 10 to 20 cm per month in four to eight consecutive months, starting earlier on going over later than the south–western monsoon months. With supplanted irrigations on 2 or 3 crops later in these areas. However it has been observed that on an all–India basis nearly 80 percent of rice is shown during June–September and the rest during the rest of season. Area were the more–season belt accounts for 46.4 per cent. (comprising Uttar Pradesh, Bihar, and Madhya Pradesh) and the multi seasons belt occupies 53.6 per cent of the area (comprising Assam, West Bengal, costal Orissa, coastal Andhra Pradesh, Parts of Tamilnadu, Karnataka and Kerala).

On an all India basis about 30 rice–based cropping pattern have been identified in different states. In the most humid areas of eastern India comprising Tripura, Manipur and Mizoram rice is the exclusive crop. In Meghalya, rice is alternated with cotton, vegetables and fruit crops, where as in Arunachal Pradesh where rice is not grown exclusively, the alternative crops being maize, Orissa and northern coastal districts of Andhra Pradesh, jute forms an important commercial crop alternative to rice. In West Bengal besides rice is grown over 49 per cent (5.3mha) of its cropped area (14.2 per cent of the all–India area) where as pulses, wheat, Uttar Pradesh rice is gross on 19 percent (4.6mha) of its cropped area and represents about 12.4 percent of the all–India area under this crop. Rice is concentrated in the eastern districts of Uttar Pradesh where the alternative crops are pulses, groundnut, sugarcane, bajra, and jowar in the decreasing order of their importance Tobacco is grown in some districts.

In Orissa, rice is grown on more than 50 percent of the area where as the alternative crops are: pulses, ragi, oil seeds, maize and small millets. In Madhya Pradesh, rice is grown in the chattisgarh area as 4.3 m ha (11.7 percent of the all India rice area) but the crop suffer because of inadequate rainfall and irrigations. The important alternatives crops of this area are: small millets pulses and groundnut. Wheat is also grown on a limited scale.

In the southern states, namely Andhra Pradesh, Tamilnadu and Kerala rice is grown in more than one season and mostly under irrigation or under sufficient rainfall together, there three states have over 6.0mha representing over 17 percent of the all–India are under rice. Important alternative crops in Andhra Pradesh are: pulses, groundnut, jowar, maize, sugarcane and tobacco. In Karnataka, the crops alternative rice are: ragi, plantation crops, bajra, cotton, groundnut, jowar and maize. In Kerala plantations crops and tapioca from the main crops alternative to rice. In Maharashtra, rice is grown mostly in the Konkan area over 1.3mha along with ragi, pulses, rabi, jowar, groundnut, sugarcane and oilseeds. In other states namely Gujrat, Jammu and Kashmir, Rajasthan and Himachal Pradesh, rice in Punjab and Haryana and to some extent in western Uttar Pradesh owing to high water–table during the monsoon season, rice has become a major crops on such areas.

The Kharif Cereals Other Than Rice

Maize jowar and bajra from the main Kharif cereals, where as ragi and small millets come next and are grown on a limited area. By and large, maize is a crop grown commonly is high–rainfall areas, or on soils with a better capacity for retaining moisture, but with good drainage. Next comes jowar is the medium rainfall regions where as bajra has been the main crops areas with low a less dependable rainfall all on light–textured soils. The extent of the area under these crops during the south–western monsoon season in maize, 5.6mha jowar (kharif) 11mha, bajra, 12.4mha. Even though these crops are spread all new the western northern and southern India, the regions of these cropping pattern are demarcated well to the west of 80 degrees longitudes (except that of maize) Ragi as a Kharif cereal (2.4mha) is mainly concentrated in Karnataka, Tamilnadu.

Andhra Pradesh which account for more than 60 percent of the total area under this crops in India. The cropping patterns based on each of these kharif cereals are discussed.

The maize–based cropping patterns. The largest area under the kharif maize is in Uttar Pradesh (1.4 mha), followed by Bihar (0.96mha), Rajasthan (0.78mha), Madhya Pradesh (0.58 mha) and Punjab (0.52mha). In four states, namely Gujarat, Jammu and Kashmir, Himachal Pradesh and Andhra Pradesh, the area under maize ranges from 0.24 to 0.28mha in each, whereas other states have much less area under it. Taking the rainfall of the maize growing areas into consideration, over 72 percent of the areas receive 20-30 cm per month of rainfall in at least two months or more during the south–westerly monsoon season.

On the all–India basis about 12 cropping patterns have been identified. They have maize as the base crop. In the maize–growing areas of Uttar Pradesh and Bihar, rice in Kharif and wheat in rabi are the main alternative crops. In some areas bajra, groundnut, sugarcane, ragi and pulses are taken as alternative crops. In Rajasthan, maize is grown as an exclusive crop in some areas, whereas at other places, it is replaced by small millets, pulses, groundnut and wheat (rabi). In some areas, bajra and rice are also grown as alternative crops. In some areas, bajra and rice are also grown as alternative crops. In Madhya Pradesh, mainly the Kharif jowar is replaced by maize, whereas rice and groundnut are also grown to a limited extent. In Punjab, maize has groundnut, fodder crops, and wheat (rabi) as alternative crops. In other states e.g. Gujarat, rice, groundnut, cotton and wheat form the alternative crops in the maize growing areas. Rice and wheat are the main alternative crops in the maize–growing areas of Himachal Pradesh, whereas in Andhra Pradesh, rice, Kharif jowar, and oilseeds are grown in these areas.

The Kharif jowar–based cropping patterns. The area under the kharif jowar in India is highest in Maharashtra (2.5mha), closely followed by Madhya pradesh (2.3mha), whereas in each of the states of Rajasthan, Andhra Pradesh, Karnataka and Gujarat, the area under this crop is between 1.0 and 1.4 mha. Jowar is mainly grown where rainfall distribution ranges from 10-20cm per month at least for 3 to 4 months of the south–westerly monsoon or is still more abundant.

On the all–India basis, about 17 major cropping patterns have been identified. In them the crop is the kharif jowar. Most of the alternative crops are also of the type which can be grown under medium rainfall.

In Maharashtra, cotton, pulses, groundnut and small

millets are sown as alternative crops. In the adjacent states of Madhya Pradesh, besides the above alternative crops, wheat and fodders are sown. In Rajasthan, wheat cotton, bajra and maize are grown in the kharif–jowar tract, whereas in Andhra Pradesh, groundnut, cotton, pulses and oilseeds form the main alternative crops. Besides cotton and groundnut, ragi is sown in the kharif–jowar tract of Karnataka whereas in Gujarat, bajra, cotton, and groundnut are the major alternative crops.

The bajra–based cropping patterns. Bajra is a more drought–resistant crop than several other cereal crops and is generally preferred in low–rainfall areas and on light soils. The area under the bajra crop in India is about 12.4 m ha, constituting an additional 1/3 area under areas receiving 10–20 cm per month of rainfall, extending over 1 to 4 months of the south–westerly monsoon.

On the all–India basis, about 20 major cropping patterns have been identified with bajra. However, it may be observed that jowar and bajra are grown mostly under identical environmental conditions and both have a wide–spectrum adaptability in respect of rainfall, temperature and soil.

Considering the cropping patterns in different states, bajra is grown along with pulses, groundnut, oilseeds and kharif jowar in Rajasthan. Gujarat has a similar cropping pattern in its bajra areas, except that cotton and tobacco are also grown. Maharashtra, besides having some areas solely under bajra, pulses, wheat, rabi jowar, groundnut and cotton are substituted for it. In Uttar Pradesh, maize, rice and wheat from the main alternative crops to this crop.

The groundnut–based cropping patterns. Groundnut is sown over an area of about 7.2 m ha, mostly in 5 major groundnut–producing states of Gujarat (24.4 per cent area), Andhra Pradesh (20.2 per cent), Tamil Nadu (13.5 per cent), Maharashtra (12.2 per cent) and Karnataka (12.0 per cent). Five other states viz. Madhya Pradesh, Uttar

Pradesh, Punjab, Rajasthan and Orissa, together have about 17.3 percent of the total area under this crop. The rainfall in the groundnut area ranges from 20–30 cm per month in one of the monsoon months and much less in other months. In some cases, the rainfall is even less than 10 cm per month during the growth of the crop. The irrigated area under groundnut is very small and that too, in a few states only viz. Punjab (16.4 percent) and Andhra Pradesh (12.5 per cent) and Tamil Nadu (13.3 per cent).

On the all–India level, about 9 cropping patterns have been identified with this crop. In Gujrat, besides the sole crop of groundnut in some area, bajra, is the major alternative crop, this tract. In Andhra Pradesh and Tamilnadu, this crop receives irrigation in some areas and rice forms an alternative crop. Under rainfed conditions, bajra, kharif jowar, small millets, cotton and pulses are grown as alternative crops. In Maharashtra, both the kharif and rabi jowar and small millets are important alternative crops. In Karnataka also, jowar is the major alternative crops. Whereas cotton, sugarcane and wheat are also grown in this tract.

The cotton-based cropping patterns. Cotton is grown over 7.6 m ha in India. Maharashtra share 36 percent (2.8 m ha), followed by Gujarat with 21 percent (1.6 m ha), Karnataka with 13 per cent (1 m ha) and Madhya Pradesh with 9 percent (0.6 m ha) of the area. Together, these four states account for about 80 percent of the area under cotton. Other cotton–growing states with smaller areas are Punjab with 5 per cent (0.4 m ha), Andhra Pradesh and Tamilnadu each with 4 per cent (0.31 m ha), Haryana and Rajasthan with 3 per cent each (0.2 m ha). Most of the cotton areas in the country are under the high to medium rainfall zone. The cotton grown in Madhya Pradesh, Maharashtra, Karnataka and Andhra Pradesh (4.8 m ha) is rainfed, whereas in Gujarat and Tamilnadu (1.93 m ha) it receives partial irrigation (16 to 20 per cent of the area). The area under cotton in Punjab, Haryana, Rajasthan and Uttar

Pradesh (0.89 m ha) gets adequate irrigation, ranging from 71 to 97 per cent of the area. These grown conditions, together with the species of cotton grown, determine the duration of the crop which may vary from about 5 to 9 months.

On the all–India basis, about 16 broad cropping patterns have been identified. In Maharashtra, Madhya Pradesh, Andhra Pradesh and Karnataka, the cropping patterns in the cotton–growing areas are mostly similar owing to identical rainfall. These patterns include jowar (Kharif and rabi), groundnut and small millets. Pulses and wheat are also grown on a limited area. In some pockets, where irrigation is available rice and sugarcane are also grown. In Gujarat, rice, tobacco and maize are grown, besides the rainfed crops, e.g. jowar and bajra.

The Rabi Season Cropping Patterns

Among the rabi crops wheat together with barley and oats, jowar and gram, are the main base crops among the rabi cropping patterns. Generally, wheat and gram are concentrated in the subtropical region in northern India. Whereas the rabi sorghum is grown mostly in the Deccan. The extent of these areas in different states is as follows.

Crop	*Area/Region (percent of the all–India area)*
Wheat 19 m ha	Uttar Pradesh (33), Madhya Pradesh (19), Punjab (13), Rajasthan (8), Bihar (7.5), Haryana (6.5), Maharashtra (5.5)
Gram 8.0 m ha	Uttar Pradesh (25.2), Madhya Pradesh (21.4), Rajasthan (20.7), Haryana (14.2)
Jowar (rabi) 6.5 m ha	Maharashtra (55.0), Karnataka (25.7), Andhra Pradesh (24.3)

The wheat and gram based cropping patterns. These two crops are grown under identical climate and can often be substituted for each other. The core of the wheat region responsible for 70 per cent of the area and 76 per cent of production comprises Punjab, Haryana, Delhi, Uttar Pradesh, and Madhya Pradesh, flanked by Rajasthan and Gujarat in the west region and Bihar and West Bengal in the east region. This area has an extensive irrigation system ranging from 85 per cent area in Punjab to 51 per cent in Bihar. The rainfall during the south–westerly monsoon is also fairly high with over 20 cm to 30 cm of rainfall in at least two out of the four months of the rainy season. However, winter showers are scattered and form less than 2.5 cm in each month from November to February.

On the all–India level, about 19 cropping patterns have been identified with wheat and 7 cropping patterns with gram. In Uttar Pradesh, maize, rice, jowar (k), small millets and groundnut form the main crops preceding wheat and gram. Generally, gram is grown on more moisture retentive soils but with little irrigation or in areas with less of rainfall. In Madhya pradesh, wheat is grown with stored moisture, with little for want of adequate moisture with stored moisture, with little irrigation and rainfall during crop period. The crop suffers heavily for want of adequate moisture with resultant low yields (57 per cent of the all–India yield). The kharif jowar, groundnut, oilseeds, cotton, small millets and fodders form the alternative crops to wheat area is under irrigation and therefore, has rice, maize, fodders, bajra and cotton as the crops preceding wheat. The area under gram in Punjab is very meagre (4.2 percent of the all–India gram area). In Rajasthan the kharif jowar fodders and bajra precede wheat, whereas gram and other oilseeds form alternative crops in winter. In Bihar, rice, maize and pulses are the main preceding crops, preceding crops, wheat in the winter–growing areas, whereas wheat and gram are the main alternative crops in winter. Rice, maize, bajra and jowar form the main preceding crops. In Maharashtra, most of the wheat crop is grown on residual moisture, bajra and other small millets or short–duration pulses form the monsoon crop in the wheat areas. Generally, heavy black cotton soils of Maharashtra and the adjacent operational difficulties and wheat is grown after the cessation of rains with stored moisture. In Maharashtra, the rabi jowar is a crop alternative to wheat.

Rabi jowar–based cropping patterns. On the all – India level, about 13 cropping pattern have been identified with the rabi jowar. Maharashtra has the largest number of these cropping patterns, where in starting with the exclusive rabi jowar, bajra, pulses, oilseeds and tobacco are grown as alternative crop. In Karnataka, small millets, groundnut, bajra, pulses and oilseeds from alternative crops to the rabi jowar. Cotton and tobacco are also in some parts of rabi–jowar area of Karnataka. In Andhra Pradesh, short–duration pulses, small millets paddy and oilseeds form the main alternative crops in the jowar area.

Plantation and Other Commercial Crops

Crops under this category include sugarcane, tobacco, potato, jute, tea, coffee, coconut, rubber and other crops, such as spices and condiments. Some of them are seasonal, some annual and some perennial. Generally, the areas occupied by them are very limited as compared with food and other crops. Nevertheless, they are important commercially. Most of them require specific environmental conditions and from the point of view of cropping patterns, they, are concentrated in some particular regions. Besides, certain horticultural crops, such as apple, mango and citrus are important. The extent of the area and the regions in which they are grown are shown below:

Crops	*Area/Region (percent of the all– India area)*
Sugarcane 2.5 m ha	Uttar Pradesh (51), Haryana (6), Bihar (6), Punjab (6), Maharashtra

	(8), Andhra Pradesh (5), Tamil Nadu (5), Karnataka(3)
Tobacco 0.427 m ha	Andhra Pradesh (48), Gujarat (19.5), Karnataka (8.7), Maharashtra (3.5), Tamil Nadu (3.5)
Potato 0.491 m ha	Uttar Pradesh (33.6), Bihar (20.4), West Bengal (13.3), Assam (5.2), Orissa (4.8)
Jute 0.778 m ha	West Bengal (60), North Eastern Region (18.7), Bihar (17.6), Orissa (6.1), Uttar Pradesh (1.7)
Coconut 1.05 m ha	Kerala (68.3), Karnataka (12.4), Tamil Nadu (9.7), Andhra Pradesh (3.5)
Rubber 0.197 m ha	Kerala (92.8), Tamil Nadu (5.0), Karnataka (1.9)
Cashew 0.264 m ha	Kerala (67.4), Karnataka (12.1), Andhra Pradesh (10.8), Tamil Nadu (9.8), Maharashtra (4.8)
Tea 0.35 m ha	West Bengal, Assam and Tripura(77), Kerala, Tamil Nadu and Karnataka (20)
Coffee 0.138 m ha	Kerala, Tamil Nadu and Karnataka (99)
All fruit crops1.8 m ha	Spread all over India
Onion 0.16 m ha	Maharashtra (18.5) Karnataka (11.7), Andhra Pradesh (12.8), Tamil Nadu (11.7), Andhra Pradesh (12.8), Tamil Nadu (11.2), West Bengal (7.6), Madhya Pradesh (7.2), Orissa (6.8), Punjab(6.2)
Chillies 0.733 m ha	Andhra Pradesh (26.9), Maharashtra (20.4), Karnataka

	(14.5), Tamil Nadu (10.0), Madhya Pradesh (5.5)`
Coriander 0.283 m ha	Andhra Pradesh (36), Rajasthan (23.6), Madhya Pradesh (11.1), Tamil Nadu (10.0)

In several sugarcane–growing areas, mono–cropping is practiced, and during the interval between the crops short–duration seasonal crops are grown. In Uttar Pradesh, Bihar, Punjab and Haryana, wheat and maize are the rotation crops. Rice is also grown in some areas. In the Southern states, namely Tamil Nadu, Andhra Pradesh and Karnataka, ragi, rice and pulses are grown along with sugarcane. In Maharashtra, pulses, jowar and cotton are grown.

In the potato-growing region, maize, pulses and wheat are the alternative crops. In the tobacco-growing areas, depending on the season and the type of tobacco-growing areas, depending on the season and the type of tobacco-growing areas, jowar, growing areas, rice is the usual alternative crop.

In the case of plantation crops, intercropping with pulses and fodder crops is common. Spices and condiments are generally grown on fertile soils. Chillies are notated with jowar, whereas onion, coriander, turmeric and ginger are grown as mixed crops with other seasonal crops.

Mixed cropping Crop Mixture are widely grown, especially during the kharif season. Pulses and oilseeds are grown with maize, jowar and bajra. Lowland rice is invariable grown unmixed, but in the case upland rice, several mixtures are prevalent in eastern Uttar Pradesh with Chotanagapur Division of Bihar and in the Chattisgarh. During the rabi season, especially in the unirrigated areas on the north, wheat and barley and wheat and gram of wheat + barley + gram are the mixtures of grain crops. Brassica and sunflower are grown mixed with gram or even with wheat. Mixed cropping was considered by researchers as primitive practice, but now many researchers regard mixed cropping as the most efficient way of using land. Several the mixtures have recently been suggested. They ensure an efficient utilization of sunshine and land. Breeders are developing plant types in pulses and oilseeds, with good compatibility with row crops.

The future of cropping patterns. With the increase in population, the irrigated area is increasing and with advances in agricultural science, most of the extensive cropping. The development in minor irrigation works has especially provided the farmers with opportunities to crop their land all the year round with high–yielding varieties. This intensive cropping will require an easy and ready availability of balanced fertilizers and plant protection chemicals and an appropriate price policy for inputs and agricultural produce.

India is a country of small farmers. In the future, the size of the holding will diminish further. The country has to produce enough for its people without deteriorating the quality of the environment.

Bibliography

1. Ahluwalia, M.S. (1978), "Rural Poverty and Agricultural Performance in India," *Journal of Development Studies,* No. 14.
2. Amit Bhaduri, *Economic Structure of Backward Agriculture,* Macmillan, Delhi, 1983.
3. Appu, P.S. Inadequacies of Politices and Programmes, *Kurukshetra,* 27(8): 16, 1977.
4. Ashok Gulati and P.K. Sharma, Government Intervention in Agricultural Markets: Nature, Impact and Implications, *Journal of Indian School of Political Economy,* Vol. 3, No. 2, April-June, 1991.
5. Azad, P. and et al., (1985), Why Mixed for Marginal and Small Farmers (A Case Study) *Indian Journal of Agricultural Economics,* Vol. XI, No. 3, p. 339.
6. Bandyopadhyaya, (1988), *The Poverty of Nations,* New Delhi Allied Publishers, pp. 4-9.
7. Bardhan (1973) On the Incidence of Poverty in Rural India in the Sixties, *Economic and Political Weekly,* Vol. 8, Annual No. Feb.
8. Bardhan, P.K. On the Minimum level of living and the Rural Poor, *Indian Economic Review,* April, 1991.

9. Bhatty, I.Z. (1993), Inequality and Poverty in Rural India in T.N. Srinivasan and P.K. Bardhan, *Op. Cit,* pp. 291-336.

10. Chandha, G.K., (1992), Non-farm Sector in Rural China: Trends and Variations in Labour Productivity, ILO/ARTEP Working Paper, New Delhi.

11. D.K. Desai, Institutional Credit Requirement for Agricultural Production 2000 A.P. Indian Journal of Agricultural Economics, Vol. XLVIII, No. 2, July-September, 1988.

12. Da Costa, E.P.W., (1971), "A Portrait of Indian Poverty", in A.J. Fonseca (ed.) *Challenge of Poverty in India*, Delhi, Vikas Publications.

13. Dandekar and Rath, Nilakantha (1971), *Poverty in India,* Poona: Indian School of Political Economy.

14. Dandekar, V.M. and N.K. Rath, *Poverty in India,* Indian School of Political Economy, 1991.

15. Dasgupta, R. A Cross Sectinal Analysis of Poverty and Undernutrition in Rural India, Working Paper No. 126 Trivandrum, Centre for Development Studies, 1981, p.1.

16. Desai (1986), *Rural Development*, Mumbai, Himalaya Publications House.

17. Eapen, Mridul (1994), Rural Non-Agricultural Employment in Kerala: Some Emerging Tendencies, *Economic and Political Weekly,* 29(21), pp. 1285-96.

18. Elango, R. (1985), *Inequality Poverty and Development in the Rural Select: A Study in the Eastern Region of Thanjavur District,* Tamil Nadu, p. 39.

19. Gagur, Keshav, Dev (180), *Extent and Measurement of Poverty in India,* Mittal Publications, Delhi.

20. Ganguli B.N. and (1976), *A Historical Genetic Perspective of the Levels of Living,* Delhi, Sultan Chand and Company, pp. 63-190.

21. Ghosh, Jayati (1995), Employment and Labour Understructural Adjustment-India Since 1991, *Indian Journal of Labour Economics,* 38(4), pp. 667-676.

22. Gupta (1995), Economic Reforms and its Impact on Poor, *Economic and Political Weekly,* Vol. 30, No. 22, pp. 1295-1320.

23. Haque, T. (1985), Regional Trends and Patterns of Diversification of the Rural Economy in India, *Indian Journal of Agricultural Economics,* Vol. XL, No. 3, p. 291.

24. Harris (1991), *Rural Transformation in India,* in Breman Mundle (ed.), New Delhi, Oxford University Press, pp. 429-449.

25. Jeyaraj, D. (1994), Determinants of Rural Non-Agricultural Employment: A Village Level Analysis of the Data for Tamilnadu, *Themes in Development Economics: Essays in Honor of Malcolm Adiseshiah,* edited by S.Subramaniam, Delhi, Oxford University Press.

26. Nayyar (1991), *Other Aspects of Poverty: Health and Education: Rural Poverty in India,* Oxford, Bombay, Oxford University Press, pp. 91-20.

27. Ojha, P.D. (1970), "A Configuration of Indian Poverty: Inequality and Levels of Living," *Reserve Bank of India Bulletin,* (January).

Index

I-58476